MINECRAFT BY CONCRAFTER:
An Unofficial Guide with
New Facts and Commands

A Feiwel and Friends Book
An Imprint of Macmillan
Minecraft by ConCrafter: An Unofficial Guide with New Facts and Commands.
Copyright © 2015 by S. Fischer Verlag. Translation copyright © 2016 by Jan Petersen.
All rights reserved. Printed in the United States of America by LSC Communications, Crawfordsville, Indiana. For information, address Feiwel and Friends, 175 Fifth Avenue, New York, N.Y. 10010.
Our books may be purchased in bulk for promotional, educational, or business use. Please contact your local bookseller or the Macmillan Corporate and Premium Sales Department at (800) 221-7945 ext. 5442 or by e-mail at MacmillanSpecialMarkets@macmillan.com.

picture credits:
Shutterstock.com: p. 2-3 © Thomas Pajot; p. 6 bottom left / p. 36 top left © Fedor Selivanov; p. 36 middle left © AstroStar; p. 36 bottom © Iakov Kalinin; p. 38 top right © canadastock; p. 38 middle right © Oliver Hoffmann; p. 38 bottom © Mapics; p. 39 top right © Marcio Jose Bastos Silva; p. 39 bottom right © Jenny Lilly; p. 236-237 © Pakhnyushchy; p. 238-239 © kasha_malasha
Fotolia.com: p. 222 top © Ben Brown; p. 222 bottom © Casey Neistat; p. 223 top © Markiplier; p. 223 bottom © Dan the Director;
All other photography © ConCrafter/divimove
All screenshots © Mojang AB

Minecraft® is a registered trademark of Notch Development AB.
The Minecraft Game is copyright © Mojang AB.

Minecraft

by *ConCrafter*

AN UNOFFICIAL GUIDE
WITH NEW FACTS AND COMMANDS

TRANSLATED BY JAN PETERSEN

FEIWEL AND FRIENDS ▪ NEW YORK

Table of Contents

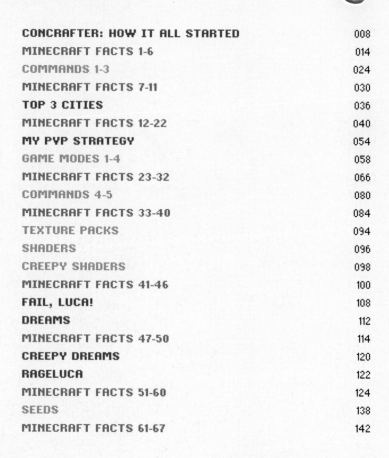

ConCrafter: How It All Started

I STUMBLED UPON MINECRAFT VIA YOUTUBE.

Back then, I followed YouTubers like DieAussenseiter and Alberto, and at some point, YouTube featured Gronkh on its start page. He ran a Minecraft "Let's Play" as the main series on his channel, and I got a kick out of this, because he had already created a real world in his videos. I immediately thought, That's cool. That's Lego for grown-ups! I have to be able to do this, too.

In the beginning, I only knew the basic principles of Minecraft: You spawn in some world, carrying nothing, and you just make your way. In the beta version, the worlds looked very different, with way fewer biomes and blocks. So five years ago, the first thing I saw was a very simple world, like the island of Majorca but cube shaped. (Now I'm suffering from nostalgia, friends.) Anyway, I just started playing; that's how I roll. When I buy a new TV set, I don't start out by reading the manual. That was my doom for the first few nights. Over and over, mobs came and killed me right away, even if I hid in a cave trying to pull something off. I started out with a lot of motivation only to die repeatedly within the first two hours because I hadn't learned how to craft things. I was really discouraged but thought, *Come on, you can do this*. I kept trying, because each time felt like a restart. *Try it again—maybe it works this time. What do you need to change?* The urge to accomplish this, to survive and create something, kept me playing.

Then I found out how to change the difficulty level. My Minecraft had been set on hard mode from the beginning. I switched to peaceful mode, no more mobs showed up, and right away, I started building a fortress for myself.

I hadn't spent much time playing before I made my first video in 2010. Back then, I made videos just for myself, with a Mac and simple software that could record only thirty seconds at a time. I recorded without sound to show certain things, like placing a lot of TNT somewhere and watching it blow up. I uploaded some of these videos to a channel no one knew about, and when they got their first clicks, I thought, *Hey, Gronkh is doing the same thing I'm doing. Okay, maybe he's a bit better at it, but actually, he's just talking over it. How about you try this yourself?*

I recorded my first commentary video with two friends half a year after my start with Minecraft. It was quite chaotic. None of us even had a proper mic. In a friend's video, you hear his mother yelling in the background all the time. My first channel was called ConqeurorLP. Apart from Minecraft, I played Sims there, but with bad quality. The sound wasn't good—totally over-modulated in parts. I really just wanted to make Minecraft videos, and for this purpose, I created my current channel, ConCrafter. I tried to be professional about it: I spent more money on software, learned more about the game, and added a FaceCam.

BEFORE YOU START COMBING THROUGH YOUTUBE LIKE A MADMAN, THE CHANNEL DOESN'T EXIST ANYMORE.

WHEN I STARTED
PUBLISHING THE
VIDEOS ON MY CHANNEL,
A LOT OF PEOPLE TOLD
ME, "HEY LUCA, YOU
ARE A GOOD TALKER."

My first *real* videos were proper Let's Plays. Actually, I'm still doing these, though now I would call them game videos over Let's Plays, which are always connected to either the gameplay or a walkthrough. When I started publishing the videos on my channel, a lot of people told me, "Hey Luca, you are a good talker." Several friends told me, "You can talk for an hour straight without floundering."

The next videos were about mods (see pg. 156). I had more fun discovering how to play with mods, learning about them beforehand, and then showing them off. In the meantime, I started editing a bit, made fewer Let's Plays, and added other mini games instead. This is how my channel changed: I only want to upload what I am in the mood for. I still think that Let's Plays are cool, but after 1,000 episodes, I would be bored stiff wandering around in the same world. I'd rather provide some change, and I guess that is what some people deem cool. There is always some variety on my channel, and they never know what comes next.

MINECRAFT FACTS

In the beginning, I produced Minecraft Facts only sporadically: When there were some cool facts, there was an episode. Now, it's a pretty large series, and here you'll get the newest facts in addition to the best facts from my videos.

Fact 1

In Minecraft, it's easy to craft a boat to putter around on the water. In real life, as in Minecraft, the boat gets damaged if it crashes at high speed into an obstacle. When I drive it into sand, the boat gets damaged.

However, when I drive it into soul sand, it doesn't. I can't explain why, but it's quite convenient if you have two houses and want to

015

travel between them. You could just line the stretch with soul sand, so the boat won't get damaged. ✖

UP TO VERSION 1.75, MOBS DON'T
BURN ON SOUL SAND DURING THE DAY

Soul sand is a block from the Nether, and the mobs like to stand on it because when they do, they don't burn. This is pretty cool when you want to pack some monsters into a mob trap. You could grab some soul sand from the Nether and pack the mobs in like a fishbowl. In version 1.75, that was still possible, but beginning in 1.8, mobs on soul sand are vulnerable to the sun and burn to bits. ✂

 # Fact 3

**IN MINECRAFT,
EVERY COW IS FEMALE**

Always. I know because you can fetch milk from all of them, in the same way you can get lava or water elsewhere. That's really convenient, since you don't have to spend forever looking for the right cow, and sometimes you *need* milk to help with toxic effects like weakness or poison.

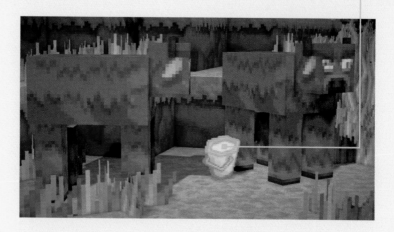

On the other hand, it's a bit unrealistic. The cows should go extinct, since for mammals, reproduction isn't really possible with only females. (Sex ed with Luca, kids.) But here you can use wheat to mate two cows, and even though they're both female, they'll make a new calf. In the end, this is Minecraft. Everything is made of cubes, so it's not very realistic to begin with. However, I do think it would be cool if there were male and female cows, with different appearances. That way, you would always have to double check: Can I get milk from this cow? ✖

Fact 4

Since hunger was added to Minecraft, you've needed food to survive. You can get food by growing wheat, carrots, potatoes, or whatever. *Or* you eat meat. Some people don't eat meat, and maybe they would rather have some bread rolls. *Or* you *could* just kill a pig. Instead of using a sword to smack the pig five or six times, use a flint and steel to set fire to the block underneath it and wait until it burns to death. Maybe that's better for the pig, as well. Or not.

In any case, when the pig burns, it drops cooked meat instead of raw, meaning you'll fill double the hunger without having to cook it in the furnace. This comes in handy, especially during survival games.

Fact 5

Are there really any fish in Minecraft? Looking at the water, at first you'd think not. You can see things like guardians, who stand watch at the water temple; or squids, which are peaceful mobs that drop the ink used to color blocks. No fish. But if you cast a rod into the

water, wait a bit, then pull it out at the right moment, you do get one, even though you can't see the fish until you've caught it. I'm sure some of you have noticed this before. ✖

Fact 6

THERE'S ANOTHER WAY TO SWITCH GAME MODES

There are four game modes: zero, one, two, and three. Zero is survival mode, Minecraft's default. One is creative mode, where you have access to every item. Two is adventure mode, a more difficult version of survival. Three is spectator mode, where you can observe and fly through all blocks.

To switch between these modes, you can use */gamemode* with *0, 1, 2,* or *3* in chat, but you can also use letters.

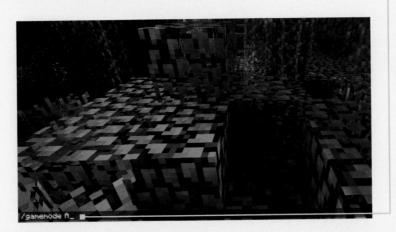

S stands for survival, *C* for creative, *A* for adventure, and *SP* for spectator. That's pretty convenient if you can't remember the numbers—for example, if you don't know which number stands for adventure mode. Just type */gamemode A* and you're done. ✂

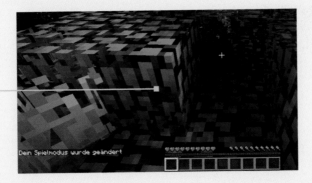

COMMANDS

In my Minecraft Facts series, I sometimes introduced commands, but I later dedicated a special series to them. Here you'll find commands I discovered recently and the best commands from my videos. Remember, you always need a command block for longer commands. In chat mode, you type: /give @p command_block. Copy the actual command into the command block.

Command 1 — Weather changes for any period specified

You can change the weather in Minecraft, but only for a limited time. The time specification is in seconds—in this case, 10 seconds. The weather changes accordingly for the specified time and then switches back to normal. You could use this to annoy your buddy: If he is complaining that it's raining yet again, you type *clear* instead of *thunder* in your chat. The weather turns fair, but just for 10 seconds, then the rain continues. ✖

Command: /weather thunder 10

Command 2

Super Mario in Minecraft

Builder: TheRedEngineer

URL: http://www.theredengineer.com/super-mario-mechanics.html

Go to this URL, copy and paste the command into your command block, and you can play Super Mario in Minecraft. The command is long. Get over it. After a few seconds, a machine appears with a sign saying "Get Items." Clicking this sign gives you nine items: bricks, coin block, mushroom block, north/south Goomba, west/east Goomba, Goomba switcher, coin, flag, and level starter. With these you can construct a complete Super Mario level in Minecraft, though I have only seen this in a video, which TheRedEngineer used to introduce this command. In my video, I only built a small level, which unfortunately doesn't really work.

Walking onto the level starter transforms your character into Mario and gives you the saturation and jump-boost effects. Jumping into coin blocks gives you coins. Mushroom blocks spawn mushrooms that cause your character to grow. Each Goomba walks in a different direction, depending on which you need. Reaching the flag finishes the level, which is celebrated with fireworks. ⚹

[ommand]

A snowball
that spawns a village

Builder: IJAMinecraft

URL: http://www.ijaminecraft.com/cmd/village_generator/

IJAMinecraft's command starts out with an incredibly tall tower of command blocks and redstone. It takes about 15 seconds for a machine to be created, and then I receive a snowball. This snowball is twinkling, which means it is enchanted. Wherever I throw the

snowball, bats spawn for a moment, then die. In their place houses begin to grow—some of them made of cobblestone, others from wooden planks. They look similar to the ones in the NPC villages. They are walkable, decorated with torches, and inhabited by NPCs. ✖

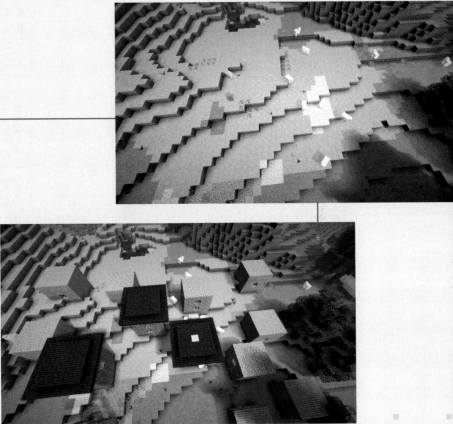

Fact 7

**THE WEATHER CHANGES
EVERY SEVEN IN-GAME DAYS**

In real life, the weather is always changing. Here in Cologne, the sun was shining just a moment ago, but now we're covered with clouds. In Minecraft, there's no completely covered sky or scattered showers, but you'll always have some clouds, with sun, rain, and snow depending on the weather. If it's raining, don't be sad. Once it stops, there won't be any more for seven days, on average. So really, for five to nine days, expect something other than rain. ✖

 **Fact 8**

As we learned already, all cows are female. Not only are they female, but they also have an unlimited milk capacity—meaning you'll get it every time. To demonstrate, I got myself a stack of buckets and

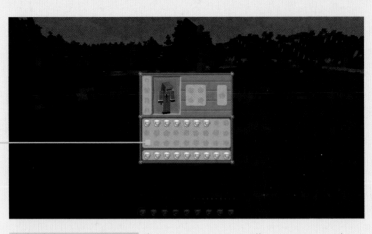

clicked the cow 16 times. The same cow gave milk every time without a break. That cow must feel really KO'd. At some point, she can't have anything left in her. ✄

Fact 9

ITEMS CAN DISAPPEAR IN CREATIVE MODE

In Minecraft, you collect items on the ground automatically—it's the same principle in survival or creative mode. However, if you have a completely filled inventory in creative mode, things act differently. If I run over an item while I am fully loaded, I can still collect the item, but it disappears right away into the Destroy Item slot. Avoid laying things on the ground when you are in creative mode and your inventory is already filled. ✄

Fact 10

As we learned already, you can change to spectator mode by typing */gamemode SP* or */gamemode 3* in chat. Spectator mode enables you to fly freely through the world, and scrolling the mouse wheel adjusts the flight speed. When I scroll up, I gain speed. By scrolling down, I can diminish my speed until I come to a complete standstill. Turning the mouse wheel *all* the way up and sprinting on top of that

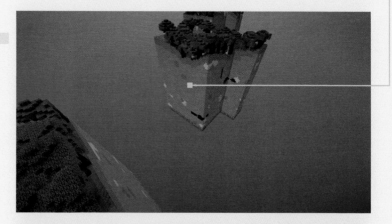

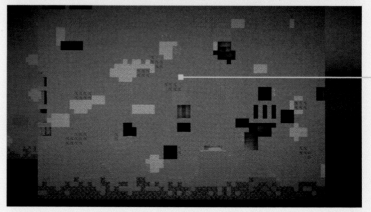

can sometimes cause so much acceleration that the game can't render the screen normally. You can use this to cheat a bit and see where to find ore, which is pretty cool! ✖

Fact 11

THE COMMAND /XP GIVES YOU EXPERIENCE POINTS

Type /xp followed by a number to give yourself experience, similar to the way bottles o' enchanting work. The highest level you can reach is 21,863. After this, you can't collect more experience, whether naturally—with a bottle o' enchanting—or through commands. Even though the chat may say you're gaining experience, the actual number doesn't change. ✖

Treat yourself to experience: /xp

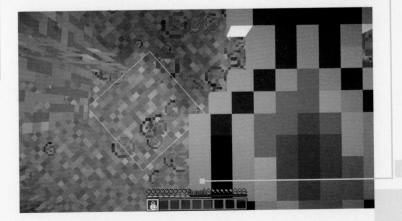

Top 3 Cities

1: London

LONDON IS ABSOLUTELY MY FAVORITE CITY.
I have been there several times and definitely want
to go back. The first time I was in London, I was with
my family, but I don't remember much. I do remember that we went to Sting's house, whom my father
idolizes. It was right at Hyde Park, a totally cool, typically English place where all the buildings look exactly
the same, but there's no tram driving by to spoil the
scene. In front of the house is a small river, and there
are taxis driving everywhere on the streets. It would
be a dream come true to live there, but houses cost
about 1.2 million—not exactly in my league.

The next time I visited London, I was there with a
language class of 10 to 20 people. We learned a lot

TOP-3

of English, for sure: It's best to learn a language in the country where it is spoken. That was my second time in London.

My best visit to London was my third. A girlfriend and I took a plane from Weeze Airport in Düsseldorf at five o'clock in the morning. When we landed, we had it all mapped out: Buy train tickets, do this, do that. We were booked. We obviously went to Piccadilly Circus, Big Ben, and the London Eye, but in between, we just rented bicycles and looked around. We winged it, letting things evolve, and by evening, we were home again. As I lay in my bed, I thought, *Since morning, I've spent the whole day in London, in a different country!* London

isn't a huge city like San Francisco, Tokyo, Shanghai, or New York—where the downtown is packed with skyscrapers—but it is still big. There are six- or seven-story buildings everywhere. You also feel very safe in London. There are cameras everywhere and patrolling guards at every square. Beyond that, there's the English culture, a pub on every corner with great burgers at each of them. There are parks all over the city, great places to relax after exploring all the interesting spots: Trafalgar Square, Piccadilly Circus, National History Museum, Big Ben, Westminster Abbey. I recommend London to everyone!

When I was in eighth grade, I wanted to do a school internship in London. I had seen movies like *Wall Street* and dreamed of working at Goldman Sachs. I never did my internship in London and math isn't my cup of tea anymore, but at the time, I had totally fallen in love with it.

2: Hamburg

Before going to college, I had a lot of free time to travel through Germany. I visited friends I'd met over the years, in Frankfurt (which wasn't really beautiful to me), Bremen, Dusseldorf, Berlin, and Munich. Then, I visited two friends, who are twins, in Hamburg. They don't live in the middle of Hamburg—more on the outskirts, near Lüneburg—but we went there for a day. It might sound weird, but I've been to Venice, and I think it's comparable to Hamburg. The thing with Venice is that everything is on a smaller scale, people are cool with one another, and the city has its own mentality. And there is water everywhere! To me, a big city should be located on the water: Cologne is on the Rhine, London on the Thames, Munich on the Isar. I don't like cities that aren't on a river or some kind of water. In Hamburg, there is Alster Lake, and the Alster runs straight into downtown. As you walk, you cross bridges everywhere, with roads leading over canals. **FOR ME, HAMBURG IS A MIX OF ANCIENT AND MODERN**—the buildings are sometimes very old and sometimes new and smooth. I think it's a perfect mixture.

3: New York City

I HAVEN'T BEEN TO NEW YORK YET, but everyone knows New York from movies like *Spider-Man* and games like Grand Theft Auto IV, and I think you can learn a lot about cities that way. In GTA IV, for example, you can take a helicopter from the Empire State Building, fly over to the Statue of Liberty, and on to the Brooklyn Bridge. I am also intrigued by Los Angeles, which I know from GTA, movies, and TV series. I'd stroll along Venice Beach, exactly as my characters did. You know these places from games, and it would be interesting to travel there and see them firsthand.

Though I only know New York from movies, games, and TV series, it is definitely a city I want to see—even with the risk that I won't like it—and I consider it one of my top three cities. It's a place that never fails to impress. It's so humongous that you feel like an ant in a haystack. When I visited Venice and London, I was never a proper tourist, like the others running around with their tourist guides. I always said, "Come on, let's discover this place by ourselves." Even though spotting the location where Spider-Man swung by would make me happy, I just don't think I could be a tourist checking places off a list. I don't think you can get to know a city by going to the tourist spots. Sure, everything there is beautiful, glamorous, and twinkling, but to discover the charm of a city, you have to explore it yourself.

Fact 12

In Minecraft, as you know from real life, cacti only grow on sand. They also hurt when you touch them, making them useful in mob traps. Use flowing water to push the mobs against cacti, then wait for them to die and drop their items. However, if you throw an item against a cactus, it disappears, no matter how durable the item might be:

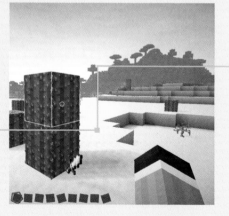

anvil, diamond sword, or feather. You can use this fact to set up a cactus like a garbage bin in your house. Throw the items against it, and they're gone. ✖

Fact 13

A TROLLEY ALWAYS POINTS SOUTH

No matter which direction the tracks are facing, a trolley always points to the south when placed. Once it starts rolling, it turns and faces the direction it's moving. ✖

IF YOU DON'T ENTER A SEED
MANUALLY, MINECRAFT USES
THE ACTUAL TIME AS THE SEED

The seed, also called the start value, is always a number. If you don't manually enter a number, Minecraft uses a start value taken from real time to generate a world. Since time is constantly changing, even by just a millisecond, this will never create the same world. The only way to generate the same world is with the same seed, which you must input yourself. ✄

Startwert: 7351943313554662853

Fact 15

AFTER YOU SPAWN, YOU ALWAYS POINT SOUTH

Landschaft wird heruntergeladen

When it comes to pointing, players are like trolleys. Check it yourself: When you create a new world and spawn (appear in the game world) you'll be looking south. When you move, you obviously control where you look, but whenever the time comes that you die, you'll find yourself looking south again. ✄

Fact 16

THE KEY COMBINATION F3 + B
SUPERIMPOSES HITBOXES

There are many key combinations in Minecraft, like *F3 + B*, which displays the hitboxes of objects. Hitboxes indicate the area around objects that enables collision with another object—or the other collision box, to be precise. For example, it shows the area where I can hit a sheep. Nothing happens if I hit any other part of a sheep outside the collision box. You can deactivate the hitboxes by pressing *F3 + B* again. ✄

Fact 17

THE KEY COMBINATION F3 + H
SHOWS ITEM DURABILITY

In survival mode, every item has a specific durability. With every block destroyed, the durability goes down one point. Usually, you can only estimate the durability of an item by looking at its bar in your inventory. You may be asking yourself, "Is there any way that I could check this? Is there not some specific function?" Yes, my

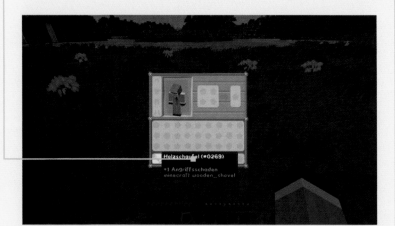

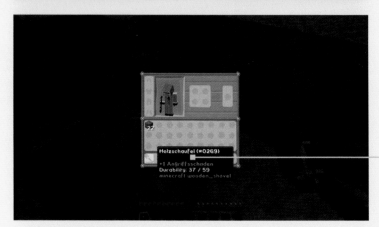

friend, there is! The key combination *F3 + H* shows the durability of each item. After mining 22 blocks, my wooden shovel has a durability of 37/59, meaning I can mine 37 more blocks before it breaks. Durability is the life of the item, and you can use this tip to check how long your items have left. ✖

Fact 18

CREEPER + LIGHTER = BAM

How to *not* explode a creeper: Set fire to the block under him so that he burns. How *to* explode a creeper: Right-click with a flint and steel on the creeper itself. He'll activate, explode, and blow everything up.

This is great for when you want the creeper to explode exactly where he is—on a slab of stone, for example. ✖

Fact 19

This fact was sent to me a while back by a viewer. I didn't believe it at first, but it works: TNT wreaks more havoc on ice than on anything else. What causes it—what exactly the reason is for this—stays a mystery, my friend, but feel free to check this out at home. You can see

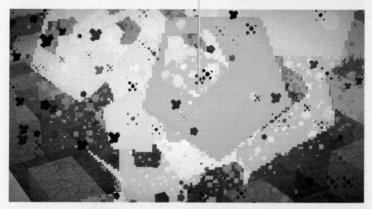

in the screenshot that the hole created by the explosion is bigger. There's nothing to be done except live with it. ✖

Fact 20

YOU CAN'T CRAFT A STONE SHOVEL WITH A NORMAL STONE BLOCK

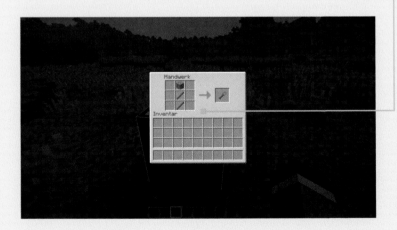

You can always craft a shovel from cobblestone. You can use a furnace to cook cobblestone into regular stone, but you can't craft a shovel from it, which is a bit confusing. It's called a *stone* shovel after all, not a *cobblestone* shovel. It's upsetting. I can craft stairs from any kind of wood, so why can't I craft a stone shovel from stone, something probably more durable than cobblestone? ✖

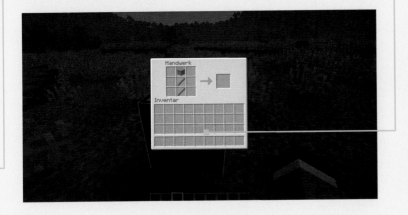

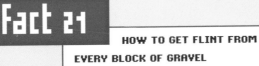

Fact 21

HOW TO GET FLINT FROM EVERY BLOCK OF GRAVEL

When you use your shovel—wood, stone, gold, or diamond—to mine a gravel block, you have a chance to get flint. As a general rule, flint drops from every three or four blocks, so your chances aren't slim, but they aren't that great, either. If you're *really* set on grabbing a lot of flint, you can enchant your shovel with Luck 3, which multiplies your chance of finding flint. I mined this group of 27 gravel

blocks with an enchanted shovel, and every gravel block gave me flint—notice that I have 27 flint in my inventory.

This doesn't only work with gravel and flint, like in this example. You can enchant a pickaxe, as well, so when you are mining ore, you might get more than one diamond. ✖

Fact 22

WHEN YOU GET ATTACKED BY A BURNING ZOMBIE, YOU START BURNING, TOO

Zombies burn during the daytime unless they're in the shade. They also burn when someone sets fire to them. Either way, that won't stop them from attacking, and if they're already lit, you'll catch on fire and take fire damage in addition to the damage from their hits. ✖

My PvP Strategy

KranCrafter

In PvP, I typically use a sword to punish—meaning I run around trying to pull people into a combo. However, in other game modes, I love to use special items.

In Bedwars, there can be a lot of different helpful items, depending on the server: parachutes, lifesaving platforms, etc.

In other game modes, like Survival Games, routes are important when collecting good equipment, and the right equipment can compensate for a skills disadvantage.

As a rule of thumb, if you are well equipped, you can win, even if you are not the best PvP player. But to make an impact, you need to have a good strategy to compensate for equipment disadvantages. Plus, a good Internet connection is always important.

KranCrafter on YouTube:
www.youtube.com/KranCrafter

Sturmwaffel

My Bedwars tactic—which I made famous, in this case—is to buy a pickaxe and rush. I don't waste time buying gear and equipment. I try to win the round as quickly as possible.

I go straight for their bases, avoiding clashes with my opponents when possible, without running away. The best-case scenario is when I meet other players on their way to the center or to their bases, where the path is only one block wide and they are easy to beat.

Sturmwaffel on YouTube:
www.youtube.com/SturmwaffelLP

Stegi

"How did you become so good at Minecraft?" I have no answer to this question; there's no perfect solution for the fighting system. Rather, it is a combination of diverse factors, from the selection of textures to strafing—the tactical avoidance of hits using direction keys. Many players underestimate game knowledge, the deeper understanding of the game's mechanics, especially in projects like VARO. Fights can be decided—independent from PvP skills, by where you set up camp, the use of fishing rods or snowballs, or the construction of complex traps. Even enchanting can lead to victory if used properly. The problem with game knowledge is that it's hard to train; it gets acquired over time. One of the most difficult disciplines is to make the right decision in stressful situations. Should I attack immediately, regenerate life first, or find a better position? Every PvP player should strive to stay detached and focused.

Experience is the key to success. The more you play, the more situations you'll find yourself a step ahead of your opponent because you've been there before. Skills like aiming, strafing, and hotkeying need time to develop.

Stegi on Youtube:
www.youtube.com/byStegi

Luca

My PvP strategy: I have none. Period. I rarely plan Minecraft PvP, and I have no plans to become any better at it. Many say, "Luca, take some PvP training lessons." Maybe when this book has been published, I will have done some research, but probably not.

It'd be okay if I were incredibly good, but right now I'm the one who can't play Minecraft PVP properly, which lets me edit things in a way I think is hilarious.

In Bedwars, I'm actually pretty good, because I can just run. Same goes for Survival Games, where you just run away in the beginning.

Avoid the center, look for something useful, and hide while the others chop each other's heads off. After everyone else is eliminated, I step up. I usually still lose—though I think I may have won at least once—and I've imagined having some kind of real tactic, but who cares? It's just a game!

Game Modes

The first online game mode I played in Minecraft was Survival Games, one of the first server games with rules and maps made specifically for online play. It originated with a YouTube event based on the *Hunger Games* movies.

For this event, 20 players spawn in a circle, all the same distance away from chests in the middle. When the countdown ends, the blocks around each player disappear and the game begins. You have to choose: Do I take the risk and run toward the chests in the hopes of grabbing a sword, or do I avoid the risk and run away? Of course, you could get meat and an apple, and the player next to you gets the sword that cuts you down. I always run away, because chests don't just spawn in the middle; they're distributed all over the map. Along with the traps.

You run onto a pressure plate, and all the blocks around you are set on fire. You run up a tower, and suddenly the stairs are missing and you fall. When there are just a few players left, the survivors are teleported together and are forced to fight until there's only one left standing. I'm recognized a lot online: "Hey, you're that guy from YouTube. Here, have my sword." I tend to win in these cases, but usually I get caught in some trap. Further development of Minecraft now allows for more complex online game modes, but

Survival Games are still clean and simple. You spawn, run to the center or run away, and survive as long as possible. ✄

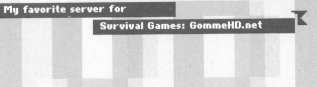
My favorite server for Survival Games: GommeHD.net

Hearing this name, you might think, Huh? Bed wars? That doesn't sound like Minecraft.

I approached this newer game mode slowly, but now I'm fascinated by how simple they've managed to keep it—similar to the SkyBlock map I'll introduce you to later. In Minecraft, you spawn next to your bed when you die. The object of this game is to destroy the beds of the opposing teams, then kill the teams once they can't respawn. Each team's bed is on its own island, and the center of the map contains a gold fountain. You can use the gold to buy better items, but you run the risk of being shot or killed. It plays much the same way as standard Minecraft: Mine a tree, make a pickaxe, use that to mine stone, then work your way up. You transform the things you get. Here you get bronze, buy a sword, use that to fight to the center, get gold, then buy a better sword to kill everyone else. ✖

My favorite server for Bedwars:
GommeHD.net

SUPER SMASH MOBS

This game mode is borrowed from Super Smash Bros., a game where the objective is to knock other players off a 2-D floating platform multiple times. This has been copied to Minecraft in a clever way, but with 3-D maps. Though there aren't as many characters in Minecraft as in Super Smash Bros., you can play as any of the mobs—spider, creeper, etc. The more damage you cause to your enemy, the farther they'll fly when you hit them and the harder it is for them to make it back to the island. This is a very hectic game mode: You're hitting each other constantly until someone tumbles off.

There is constant action, and even if you're not afraid of dying, you'll be tense the entire time.

I came across Super Smash Mobs as I was looking for new servers. Previously, I'd played a lot on the HiveMC server,

and I thought it was the best. But the management of HiveMC was weird, and a lot of people got banned. When I found the Mineplex server, its main advertised game was Super Smash Mobs.

My favorite server for Smash Mobs: Mineplex.com

HIDE 'N' SEEK

Hide 'n' Seek is very different from Super Smash Mobs. You don't kill your enemies by shoving them off platforms; you hide. It's a lot more relaxed, because you don't have to focus on the game all the time. Watch a video or soccer, or drink a cup of coffee.

In Hide 'n' Seek, there are hiders and seekers, cops and robbers, cowboys and Indians. The hiders don't spawn with their Minecraft skin, as regular players would. You either choose or are assigned a block: bookshelves, fences, stairs, snow, anvils—things that stand out from less noticeable blocks like dirt.

Hiders start by hiding somewhere on the map, and at first, there is only one seeker looking for them. When the seeker finds and kills a hider, the hider automatically morphs into a seeker. If you survive as a hider until the end, you get a lot of points. If you find hiders as a seeker, you get a few points. If you don't find anyone, you get no points.

My favorite server for
Hide 'n' Seek: HiveMC.com

I think this game mode is really cool when you Skype with friends, where you can give each other hints. You can tell your friend you are in a house, but they don't know you're not *inside* the house, but *on top of* it, disguised as a roof tile.

I always use Hide 'n' Seek when I'm talking about serious topics—for example, if there is something I don't agree with that is happening in the world. For this, you definitely wouldn't choose a game mode where you're always busy. You want one where you're disguised as a block and squatting in some corner, hoping not to be found. However, sitting still isn't really my cup of tea. I can't just place myself in one spot and wait for a round. I'm always running around, hyped up on adrenaline, and even then I'm often not found. In most cases, you aren't found right away, as long as you take time to think and don't disguise yourself as a bookshelf in the middle of a field. ✖

Fact 23

In creative mode, you can use an anvil and one experience point to name a spawn egg *Grumm*. Whatever you choose—let's say a sheep—will spawn upside down. "Grumm" has been a Minecraft employee since 2012 as a member of the Bukkit team. Like other employees at Mojang, he programmed a special function for his name in version 1.6.1. Grumm himself stands upside down in the game. A spawn egg with the name *Dinnerbone* has the same effect. ✄

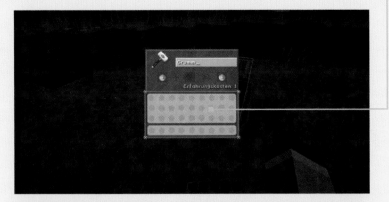

This fact uses the same principle as *Dinnerbone* and *Grumm* but only works with sheep. If you name the spawn egg *jeb_,* it will create a sheep that changes colors. Small sheep change the color of their wool permanently, a fact easily visible within a bigger flock of jeb_ sheep. All this derives—as was the case for Grumm— from a Mojang employee, Jens Bergensten, whose Internet handle is jeb_. ✵

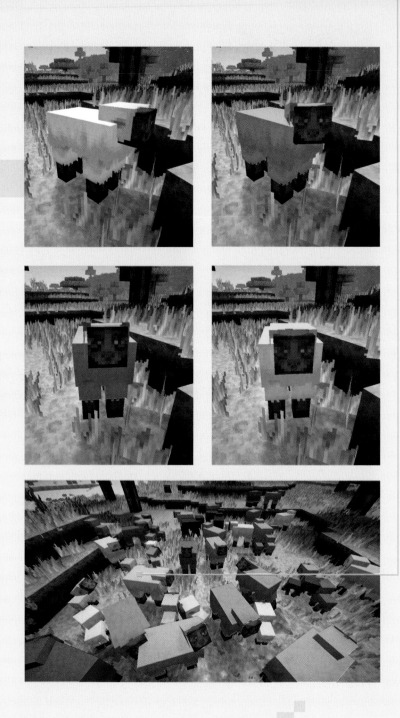

In Minecraft, you can right-click to interact with certain items, but not when you are falling. However, when you are airborne, you *can* write in a book —bringing the entire game to a grinding halt: time, animals, chat, everything. This makes no sense to me. Why would

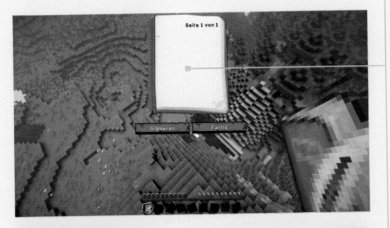

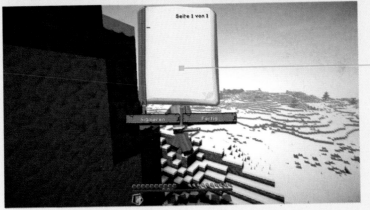

writing in a book cause me to stop in midair? In theory, I could write an entire book while falling.

Why am I telling you this? I have no clue. So many Minecraft facts are useless knowledge, and this one is no exception. ✖

Fact 26

PLAYERS CAN PASS BETWEEN FENCES AND STONE WALLS

Wooden fences and stone walls do not connect into a continuous boundary. A small slot remains between them, and even though it doesn't look like it, you can fit. This is thanks to the hitbox, which—as I said before—you can see with *F3 + B*. You can use this fact to make secret pathways online where, at first glance, you might not expect to fit. ✖

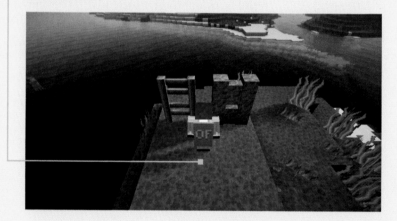

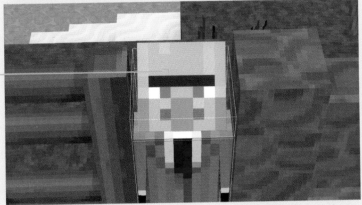

Fact 27

The babies of all peaceful mobs—like sheep, pigs, cows, or chickens—are pretty easy to spawn if you know this little trick: Just click an adult animal with that animal's spawn egg. Unfortunately, this trick doesn't work with zombies, the only hostile mobs who can spawn babies.

I noticed this when I wanted to spawn a lot of sheep on a single block. When I started getting rid of the sheep, I realized I was hitting a bunch of babies. ✖

Fact 28

SINGLE RAILS ALWAYS ALIGN NORTH-SOUTH

No matter which direction I'm looking when I place a rail, it is always aligned north to south. Of course, when I place them next to one another, they connect logically. ✖

Fact 29

**ALL ITEMS FALL AT
THE SAME SPEED**

To demonstrate this fact, I constructed a setup. On one side is a feather, a lightweight item; and on the other side is an anvil, a heavy

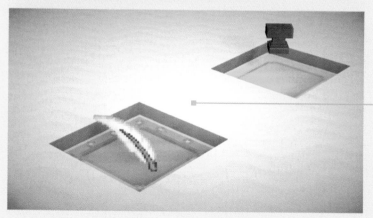

item. Not all items weigh the same, since some pressure plates are only activated by heavier items, but when I press the button and the blocks are pulled aside, the feather and anvil fall at the same speed. I think it would be cooler if heavy items fell faster, but as is, all items fall at the same speed. ✄

Fact 30

SAND AND GRAVEL FLOAT ABOVE LILY PADS

When you place lily pads on the water's surface, they take up a whole block. As a player, I can walk over them, but I can't place a block just above them. I have to place it one block up, giving the impression that sand and gravel—which fall when placed in the air—float above lily pads. In earlier versions, sand would stay in the air after

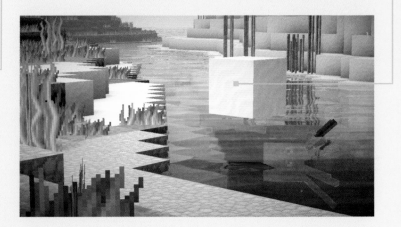

the lily pad was destroyed, but now the sand falls without getting destroyed. ✂

Fact 31

A BLOCK OF TNT UNDER AN ANVIL DOESN'T CAUSE DAMAGE

When you light a block of TNT, it takes a short time to explode. If you want to troll someone on a server, place an anvil above the TNT before you light it. During the explosion, the anvil will fall into the TNT block, absorbing all block damage and reducing the damage

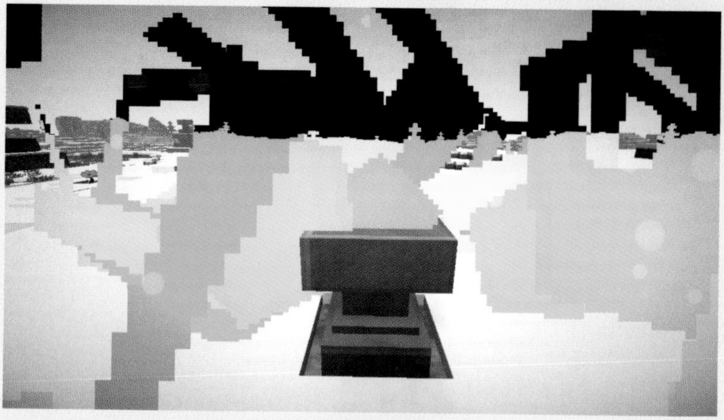

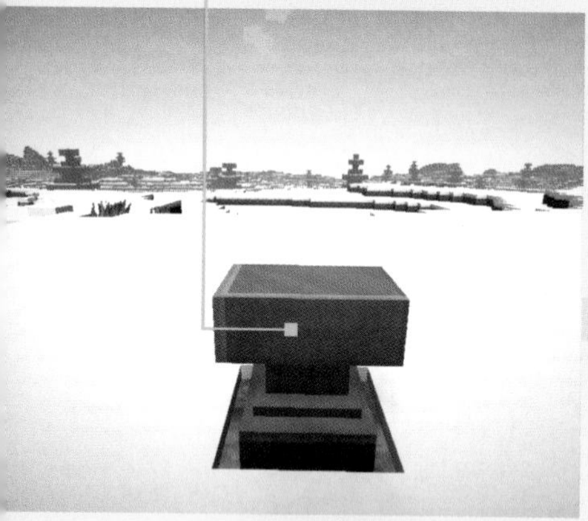

to the player drastically. I placed myself right next to it and lost just half a heart, when at that distance, I should have died.

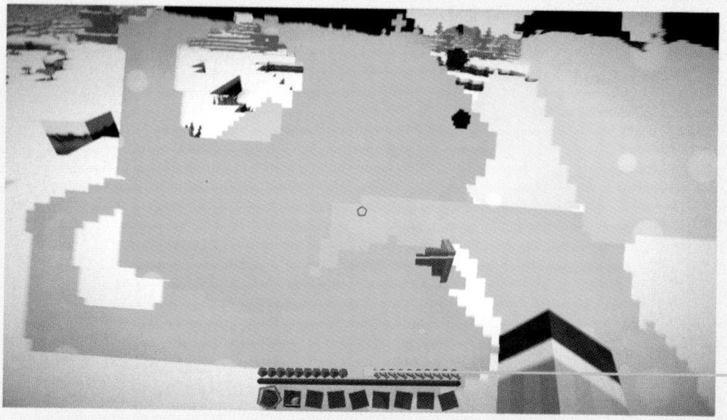

Fact 32

I introduced this in an earlier facts episode but thought it had been changed since. I just found out about it again; I didn't know that it was still possible. (Luca can still learn something new!) Unlike with other plants, there is a thin layer of air between cacti and water, so they can survive underwater. It doesn't matter if they stick out or are fully submerged, as long as they are planted on sand, like usual. ✖

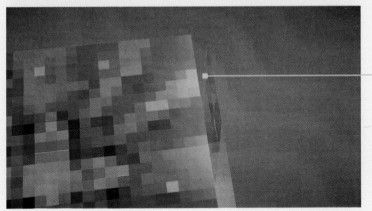

Builder: IJAMinecraft

URL: http://bit.ly/1IGxURj

As usual with IJAMinecraft's commands, a machine appears after activating the command. "This machine is fully assembled" appears in the chat window. The sign on the machine says, "Right click this sign to get your items." In this case, the only item is an instruction manual, which says a natural disaster will occur every 15 minutes, or alternatively, you can use the book to create one manually, which

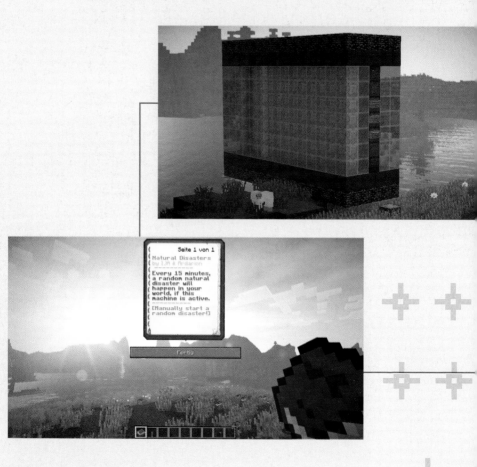

will alter your player score. So what does this do? On the spot where I triggered a catastrophe, poisonous gas was released. If I stand in or next to it, I'm poisoned. When I triggered it again, fire fell from the sky and lit the area in flames. This command doesn't add a lot

of items, but it seems pretty comprehensive; these are just two of the events this command can create. There's still a lot I don't know. The meaning of life, for example. ✂

Command 5 Chicken rides chicken

Command: /summon Chicken ~ ~ ~ {Riding:{id:Chicken}}

With the riding command, you can tell one mob to ride on top of another one. The first mob sits on top of the second, so in this case, a chicken spawns riding another chicken. Strangely, the upper chicken always flaps its wings, but they don't fly away. This command is possible with all other mobs. For example, you could place a ghast on top of a giant. ✂

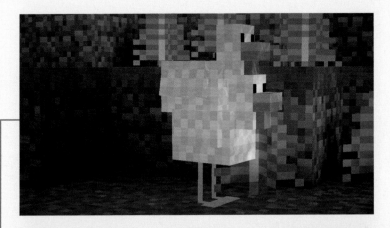

Fact 33

SNOWBALLS CAUSE A LOT OF DAMAGE TO BLAZES

The Nether is essentially the hell of Minecraft, so blazes are fiery mobs, well, straight out of hell. It might make sense to fight blazes with a sword—depending on the sword—but it's much easier to use snowballs. Normally, snowballs only push mobs and players without causing damage. But snowballs (cold) do a lot of damage to blazes (hot). ✄

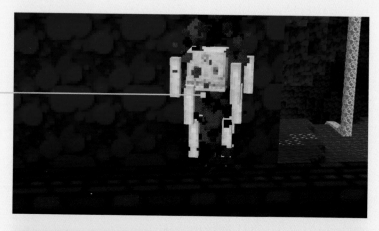

Screenshot gespeichert unter
2015-05-18_18.33.49.png

Fact 34

All mobs become invisible when you hit them with a splash potion of invisibility. Most mobs become completely invisible, including mooshrooms and sheep in later versions. However, you can still see the eyes of invisible spiders and the bows of invisible skeletons. I don't know if there's a way to change this; I can't. ✖

Werfbarer Trank der Unsichtbarkeit

Fact 35

ALL CHICKENS
ARE HENS

Quick round of biology with Luca: Roosters have combs on their
head and don't lay eggs. In Minecraft, all chickens look the same,
lay eggs, and have no combs on their head. This means there are no

roosters in Minecraft, which I would love to see them change. I want cows that don't give milk and chickens that don't lay eggs.

Again, I don't understand how chickens reproduce. Are all hens lesbians? Can they fertilize their own eggs? What is going on? ✖

Fact 36

In real life, spiderwebs are sluggish and sticky—the better for catching flies. It's similar in Minecraft. Any item stuck in a spiderweb falls at a much slower speed. You can use this to construct traps: The player walks into a trap, falls into the spiderweb, and takes a long time to reach their agonizing death. Cruel, yes, but first-rate. ✕

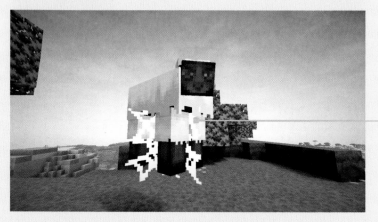

Sand and gravel are the only blocks that fall after being placed in midair. When these blocks fall through a spiderweb, they emerge as an item and not as the full block. In a way, the blocks are being

filtered as they pass through. During their transformation, they do not show the cracks that are created when mining them regularly. ⌗

Fact 38

IT RAINS ABOVE THE CLOUDS

In real life, rain and snow come from clouds. In Minecraft, it rains and snows below and *above* the clouds. You can test this by using */toggledownfall* to change the precipitation, which changes

regardless of altitude. When you fly above the clouds, you'll see it's raining and snowing there, too. ✖

Fact 39

A SAND BLOCK FALLING THROUGH A SPIDERWEB WON'T BE DESTROYED BY TNT

We already learned what happens when a sand block falls through a spiderweb. When a TNT block explodes while the sand block is in the web, every block—including the spiderweb—will take damage except the sand block. Even when the spiderweb is destroyed, the sand block falls like normal, which you can see in the screenshot. ✖

Fact 40

To prove this fact, I placed a spiderweb block over Steve. Behind him, I placed metal blocks that serve as a measuring stick with the default texture pack. You can see in the screenshot that his feet are on the same level as the first line in the second block. According to Mojang, a block is roughly three feet tall, which means Steve jumped 1.25 blocks—about four feet. From a standing position, that's quite a feat; even Michael Jordan didn't get much higher. This would easily qualify Steve as an Olympic athlete. ✖

Texture Packs

THESE ARE MY FAVORITE TEXTURE PACKS. I am using a shader in all the screenshots, because it makes them look even better.

3

PIXEL DAYDREAMS
I saw this texture pack on Palokos's channel. It reminds me a bit of Terraria: The dirt looks exactly the same. ✖

Palokos on YouTube:
www.youtube.com/PalokosDoesMinecraft

2

SIMPLE PIXEL
This 16x16-pixel texture pack is very simple. It reminds me a lot of the default texture pack. The color range is similar, but the details are extremely reduced. Leaves consist of only three squares, and the dirt has almost no detail at all. ✖

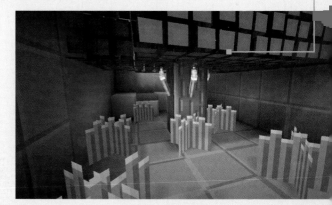

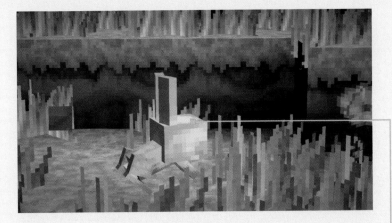

1 SPHAX PUREBDCRAFT

The Sphax texture pack comes in different resolutions, ranging from 16x16 to 256x256. I use 32x32 pixels because I think Minecraft should stay pixelated, even when using a texture pack.

I've used Sphax since I started playing Minecraft. It is one of the most popular texture packs worldwide, and rightfully so, because everything in this pack feels right. It's simple, a bit like a comic, and the details and coloring are the best.

Even though Sphax is my absolute number one, I still switch my texture pack every now and then, because it gets boring. It's like clothing: Even if a sweater fits, you start looking for a new one after a while. ✖

Shaders

IN THE PAST, I LIKED MINECRAFT BETTER WITHOUT
SHADERS, because it was simpler. Now, after buying a new PC,
I started appreciating the shader effects, so here are my two
favorites.

CHOCAPIC13 V3 ULTRA SHADER

2

Chocapic13 V3 Ultra Shader is a completely different animal, com-
pared with the KUDA-Shader. Water and leaves move, and the sun
reflects on the water, but everything is much more saturated, with
stronger illumination and sharper details. Not everyone is going to
love this right away, but it makes a cool contrast to the KUDA-Shader
and follows what made shaders so relevant in the past: more colors
and more shadows. Even I cast a shadow.

KUDA-SHADER V5 ULTRA

Of all the shaders I've seen, I like this one the most. Most people expect more color. Most YouTubers who make Minecraft videos use heavily saturated shaders. I like the KUDA-Shader V5 Ultra because it is realistic. When the sun rises in the morning, everything is hazy and gloomy, like a real sunrise. The distant landscape is darker, like it's in shade. During the day, the sun looks great: When you look

directly into it, light particles form. When I look away, I'm illuminated differently. The leaves move, and both the sun and landscape are reflected in moving, glistening water.

Creepy Shaders

NAELEGO'S CEL SHADERS 1.0.4

Look at this chicken. Look at this crazy chicken! This shader looks really sick. Every block is completely outlined: mobs, grass, myself, everything. This looks really weird from a long distance. There are no mistakes in the background; it's supposed to look this way. If you activate the black-and-white filter in the super secret settings, you'll look like a comic book. Very strange!

ACID SHADERS R5

I've only used this shader once for a video. When I see something like this, I get a headache right away. As long as I look down at the ground and mine blocks, it doesn't matter, but as soon as I raise my head, everything changes: The world spins, the mountains in the background flip, and everything bends upward like a wave, then drops down again. It's difficult to know which direction you're running or how the terrain is laid out. This is definitely my number one creepy shader, but I have to switch it off, right now. Gotta delete this crap.

Fact 41

TURN A MOOSHROOM
INTO A NORMAL COW

Mooshrooms appear in mushroom biomes. Right-clicking a mooshroom with shears turns it into a normal cow. Like a sheep, which loses its wool through shearing, the mooshroom loses its mushrooms and becomes a normal dairy cow. After being sheared, the mooshroom

drops five mushrooms but can no longer provide free mushroom soup, and there's no way to transform the new cow back into a mooshroom. So, if you happen to be walking with shears, don't right-click near mooshrooms. They're really rare. ⁌

Fact 42

You can see from the screenshot that zombies burn, except that little rascal. Though the baby zombie is just a copy of the normal zombie, he can't burn during the day—much like a helmeted zombie. I guess because he's well behaved. ⌗

Fact 43

It's pretty common knowledge that chests can only be opened if they don't have a block above them. There are a few exceptions to the rule, though: glass, leaves, and any kind of fence. Not to mention, of course, that you can open the chest while you're standing on it. You could use this to build a tree house from fences, leaves, and chests, or to hide a chest in the trunk of a tree. If you cover it with leaves, no one can see it, but anyone who knows it's there can open it. ✖

Fact 44

The giant was added to Minecraft but was never really implemented or fully realized. He doesn't appear in boss fights or spawn naturally. The only way to get a giant is the command *summon Giant*. After spawning, the giant just hangs out, standing motionless. He won't attack, even if you attack him, and when he dies, he only drops experience. When you hit the giant on his head or arms, you are essentially hitting a void, since the hitbox only covers his lower body. ✄

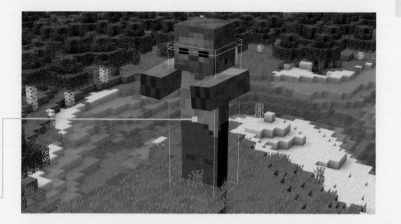

Create a giant for yourself: /summon Giant

Fact 45

ZOMBIES ARE DAMAGED BY A SPLASH POTION OF HEALING

Zombies are undead, so potion effects are inverted from ones for the living. If you heal zombies, they take damage. If you hit them with a splash potion of damage, they heal.

Fact 46

GIANTS ARE HURT BY SPLASH POTIONS OF DAMAGE

Even though the giant looks like a big zombie, he reacts to potions normally: He is healed by a potion of healing and hurt by a potion of damage. Keep in mind that for the potions to have any effect, they must hit the lower part of his body. ✖

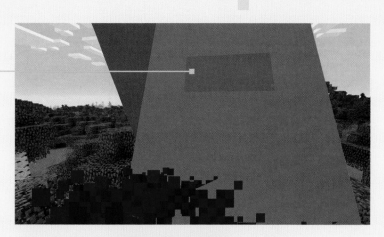

Fail, Luca!

HERE I'LL PRESENT THE BIGGEST FAILS that ever happened to me in Minecraft.

MY YARO DEATH. IIn the second season, I was on a team with LPmitKev, and our tactic was to run away from the start, dig in somewhere, and hide. It worked like a charm, and we survived for several minutes.

LPmitKev on YouTube:
www.youtube.com/LPmitKev

FOR THOSE DON'T KNOW YARO: THE NAME IS A SHORTENING OF VANILLA ROLEPLAY. IT IS LIKE SURVIVAL GAMES, BUT THERE ARE BOXES ONLY IN THE CENTER, NOT THE REST OF THE WORLD.

After 15 minutes, the session ends automatically, and a plug-in kicks you off the server. After eight minutes, we wanted more. We didn't want to stay underground the entire time—we wanted to show off, too. We were sure the other players had run in different directions and nobody was around, so we started digging further in search of items. This was a fatal error. AviveHD and GommeHD were sneaking, so we couldn't see their names. Both of them dug toward us, and we tried to fight back but

108

got ourselves killed. We could have taken one of them with us, but in the end, we died trying.

I had spent so much time preparing for VARO. It was a giant project; everyone was really excited and had planned to accomplish so much. I was shocked and disappointed.

AviveHD on YouTube:
www.youtube.com/AviveHD

GommeHD on YouTube:
www.youtube.com/GommeHD

THE HARDCORE BEDWARS CHALLENGE

In Minecraft, you move with WASD and use the mouse to look in the direction you want to run. When I visited my friend KranCrafter we shared the controls: I handled the keyboard, KranCrafter the mouse. This is the Hardcore Bedwars Challenge.

Gold spawns in the middle of the map and is the essential resource. We ran to the center, collected gold into the double digits, and ran back along the narrow path to our main island. On this tiny path, you are quite vulnerable, and there is no safety net. If another team

KranCrafter on YouTube:

www.youtube.com/KranCrafter

shows up with arrows, they can take down anyone easily. We ran as fast as possible to avoid that, not coordinating or anything. We were in permanent fear that someone would show up and attack us. When I play by myself, I jump in a slightly unusual way: I run forward

with WASD and skip at an angle over curves. When we encountered a curve, I did that, but KranCrafter pointed the mouse normally. KranCrafter pointed to the right, I jumped, and we fell to our deaths. Here's the embarrassing thing: This happened twice, and both times we had really good equipment. The second time was pure stupidity; we hadn't learned our lesson.

Dreams

I am afraid of heights. I wouldn't call it vertigo, because I think flying or looking out of a window in a tall building is totally cool, but when I sit on a Ferris wheel and look down, I start asking how long it'll be until I'm back on the ground. Just once, I want to skydive. I want it to be somewhere really cool, not in some field. Maybe somewhere abroad, where there is something to see, like a beach or an ocean. Skydiving is a dream I really think I'll do.

This may sound a bit weird at first, but I would love to be a knight in shining armor. I don't *want* anyone to be in an emergency or attacked, for sure, but when people are in need, I'd love to help.

> BACK IN ELEMENTARY SCHOOL, I WAS A PEER MEDIATOR. YOU DON'T SEE ASSAULTS OR ANYTHING LIKE THAT. YOU HANDLE ISSUES LIKE SPILLED MILK.

In my everyday life, I'm not some jerk who kicks a walking stick out from under a granny. I was raised to pick up the cane if she drops it by accident. Or, like five days ago, I was sitting on a train completely exhausted but offered my seat to an elderly man with a broken foot when there was no other seat available. I think everyone should be like this. Even with small gestures like that, I try to do my part to better society. I may sound weird, but if the world could be a bit nicer, everything would be more beautiful.

A lot of people don't want to hear their own voice. When they do—in WhatsApp voice mails, for example—they often can't believe it's them. Because of my videos, I hear my voice so often that I'm used to it. I actually find it rather amusing to listen to my own voice. That's why I'd love to record a voice for a video-game character or a character in an animated movie. I think it would be really fun to see a different character with my voice, and I'd watch whatever they were in all the time.

I've driven a Jet Ski several times already, and it was always fun. My best time was in Bulgaria because the weather cooperated. It's my dream to drive a Jet Ski like in a GTA V mission. In one mission, you have to kidnap Michael's daughter from a party boat and shake off pursuers. To accomplish this, you speed through the narrow canals between Los Santos houses. I'd absolutely love to drive a Jet Ski through a city. I have no clue if Los Angeles is like this—unfortunately, I haven't been there yet—but if there is any resemblance, I will definitely do it.

Those are some things I'd like to do in the foreseeable future. It's difficult to know when I could be a knight in shining armor, and I don't know anything about being a voice actor, but maybe something will come up. I guess skydiving or driving a Jet Ski will be next.

Fact 47

WITCHES CAN'T DIE FROM BURNING

In Minecraft, witches can't be killed by burning, unlike in the Middle Ages, when they really were. It doesn't matter if she's set ablaze with lava or fire; she'll take a potion of fire resistance as soon as she starts burning. The same goes for other negative effects: Underwater, she'll drink a potion of underwater breathing. She will always heal herself from negative effects that might hurt her. The only way you can kill a witch is with a strong weapon.

Fact 48

No matter the type of stone stairs—
cobblestone, sandstone, or quartz—
exploding creepers don't cause damage
to blocks, mobs, or players that are
beneath them, except for the stairs,
which are destroyed. If the creeper is

115

standing on wooden stairs, the explosion causes only a little damage to surrounding blocks. ✕

Fact 49

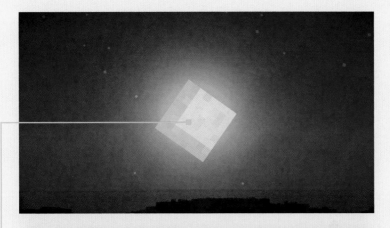

The moon determines the spawn rate of slimes: A lot of slimes spawn under a full moon, but none spawn under a new moon. A full cycle takes eight Minecraft nights, which means it takes nearly three real-world hours for the moon to change once. ✄

Fact 50

**YOU STOP TRADING WITH VILLAGERS
WHEN THEY START BURNING**

You can trade with Minecraft villagers. If the villager steps into lava or is set on fire by another player while trading, they start to burn, and you'll be kicked out of the trading screen. Burning villagers is

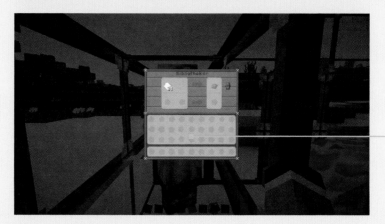

118

basically like killing villagers, so if you needed something urgently, you have a problem. ✄

Creepy Dreams

THESE ARE THE DREAMS I HAVE IN BED AT NIGHT, dreams I don't want to have again and I hope never come true..

When I was II years old, I watched *Scream*. I knew I wasn't allowed to see it, and you really shouldn't when you are young, but I did. That night, I dreamed I woke up in a warehouse. There was wood lying everywhere; it looked like a factory. At the other end of the warehouse stood Ghostface—the character from the movie—holding a knife in his hand. He began to move slowly toward me. Of course, I wanted to stand up and run away, but as most of you know, you don't make any progress in dreams like this, despite all your effort. You move wobbly and slowly or you don't move at all, while everyone else moves at normal speed.

Somehow I got away and reached an elevator. Inside, I pressed the button for another floor, but the door wouldn't close. Ghostface stepped inside the elevator and killed me.

I had the same dream six years later in Minecraft. I didn't dream in Minecraft, but I had a dream that I ran through the *Scream* nightmare with characters from Minecraft.

At the time, I was constructing mob traps: huge spaces without light, because dark rooms spawn zombies, endermen, and other monsters. I played until I fell into bed. The mob trap probably reminded me of the *Scream* nightmare, so after falling asleep, I woke up in a dark hall with a high ceiling. I wasn't a Minecraft character, but I was surrounded by Minecraft monsters: zombies, spiders, and skeletons. This time, it wasn't Ghostface but an enderman—focused on me and holding a knife. Again, I tried to run away and escape through an elevator, and once again, the elevator didn't move. Then I woke up.

121

RageLuca

I HAD MY BIGGEST FREAK-OUT during a beach-soccer tournament when I was 15 years old. The tournament was played in groups of four, and we were on the youth team. We played against younger kids, and we were clearly better: We had the physical advantage, executed dream passes, and worked out scoring chances while they stood shoulder-to-shoulder in the back. At one point, while we were pelting them with shots, they all ran forward and scored while we stood on the other side of the field in front of their goal.

Usually I am a quiet kind of guy, except when something just isn't right. Then I go really ballistic. I know that in soccer, sometimes you just defend yourself for the whole game, get balls slammed into the goalpost, and lose 3-0 in the end. I have nothing against that. Sure, you're grumpy after a game like that, but mostly toward yourself. But when it is really unfair, like that beach-soccer game, I get really upset. We lost the semifinal 1-0 and got all riled up—one guy kicking the ball away, another literally hitting the ground. When I get upset, I have to hit something to vent my rage. In this case, it was the post of the small beach-soccer goal. I kicked it as hard as I could.

Never do this! Not even with shoes on! Never kick the goalpost! (And if you really have to, do it straight with cleats.) You damage everything this way. If you get really excited, kick the sand or some grass. I didn't visit a doctor after the tournament. I thought if I put some sports gel on it and cooled it, that should work. It was two years before I went to an orthopedist, where I found out my stunt had caused an oblique pelvis position from always dragging my right foot.

The doctors had to prescribe insoles. Everything really added up, and all because of such crap—because of an unfair game and stupid 11-year-olds.

RageLuca is always connected to soccer, and it applies to the **FIFA** video games. When I see that my opponent is better, I accept it. But that wasn't the case here. I led 1-0 the entire game, playing offensively like in Barcelona vs. Glasgow Celtic. In the last attack, in the 90th minute, my opponent scored and blocked my advancement in the next league. I slammed my controller against my television. You can still see it on the screen, and you can feel it in the corner if you run your finger across it. The controller still has scratch marks, and the L2 button was ripped out. This is what happens when you play FIFA, the game that destroys friendships! Recently, I got myself a ball made from fabric, so I can kick it against the door or walls without destroying anything else.

IT'S NOT RAGELUCA, but there was another situation where I lost my self-control. I was playing a game, maybe even Minecraft, and got so startled by something unexpected that I knocked over a bottle of unfiltered apple juice. This happened in my old apartment in Bielefeld, where I had a wooden floor with white carpet—now stained green.

Fact 51

THE COMMAND /KILL @E KILLS ALL ENTITIES

With this command, you can instantly become a mass murderer. */kill @e* kills all entities, meaning not only mobs but also items like armor stands. To my chagrin, I found that this command doesn't spare me, either. This is useful when you have spawned too many mobs and the game is about to crash. Plus, every animal will be accounted

for in chat: sheep killed, rabbit killed, cow killed, etc.

All mobs and players drop items as usual, along with experience bubbles. ✖

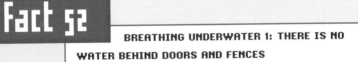

Kill all creatures: /kill @e

Fact 52

BREATHING UNDERWATER 1: THERE IS NO WATER BEHIND DOORS AND FENCES

In Minecraft, a door is two blocks tall, doesn't despawn underwater, and has empty space—meaning it doesn't occupy a whole block. This empty space is filled with air, even underwater, and is exactly the same size as a Minecraft player, so you can use it to breathe. The characteristics are the same with any kind of door: acacia, birch, etc. The same principle also applies to fences if you build them two blocks high.

This is handy for diving over long distances or exploring a water temple without using a potion. ✖

If you don't have wood at hand or aren't in the mood to craft a door, you can grow some sugarcane. Similar to doors and fences, it only occupies part of the block, and the rest is filled with air, allowing us to pass through and breathe underwater. It's best to keep one of the three—a door, a fence, or sugarcane—with you, though you could always just plant the sugarcane next to the water and grab it when you need it. ✖

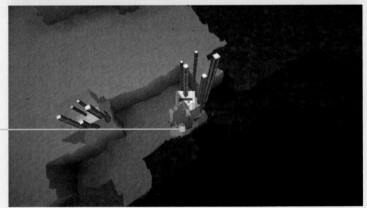

Fact 54

A GRUMM BABY ZOMBIE FLOATS ONE BLOCK ABOVE THE GROUND

As we learned before, a mob named *Grumm* will be turned upside down. You can also achieve this effect using an anvil and name tags. When you give a baby zombie the name Grumm, it turns upside down but hovers one block above the ground. This looks a bit buggy but happens because baby zombies have the same hitbox as regular zombies. If you reverted the baby zombie back to normal, its hitbox would be taller than it is. When upside down, it has to float or the hitbox would be stuck in the ground. ✖

When I light a TNT block underwater, it doesn't cause any block damage. If I put the TNT on sand before lighting it, the TNT glitches

and causes marginal damage to nearby blocks and mobs. Regardless, if you find a lot of TNT underwater, don't worry about setting it off. It won't destroy any blocks. ⌗

**BEACONS SHINE THROUGH
SOME BLOCKS**

A beacon block will emit a beam and provide powers (like speed) when placed on nine blocks of iron, gold, emerald, or diamond. Solid blocks like dirt or stone will block the beacon. However, the beacon will shine through some blocks: glass, stained glass, daylight sensors, enchantment tables, chests, ender chests, anvils, and beds. You can use this to create glowing chests, shining anvils, or change the color of the beacon with stained glass. ✕

VILLAGERS, BATS, AND
BABY MOBS DON'T DROP XP

Peaceful mobs don't fight back when attacked but will drop experience points, unless they are a villager, a bat, or a baby mob. When you're killing villagers, I guess you're killing people like you. Steve is a lot like a villager. Baby mobs aren't fully grown, and it takes fewer hits to kill them, but they're babies! You shouldn't be hitting them! I guess you don't get experience points from bats because there aren't any baby bats. ✖

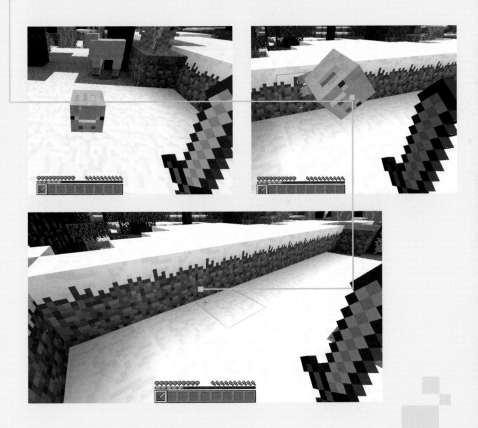

Fact 58

YOU CAN MIX THE COLORS OF A BEACON

As we learned before, you can change the color of a beacon's light using stained glass. Yellow turns the beacon yellow, green to green, blue to blue, and red to red. If you stack stained glass on top of one another, you can mix the colors. Red and green create brown, blue and yellow create green, and red and yellow create orange. It's just like mixing colors on a palette. ✖

Fact 59

APART FROM OCELOTS AND VILLAGERS, BABY MOBS AND ADULT MOBS HAVE THE SAME HEAD SIZE

I have no idea why it was coded this way. The body of baby mobs is smaller, except for the head. For some reason, this isn't the case with villagers and ocelots—maybe because it would be too strange. This is a baby villager. Imagine it with such a huge thing on its neck; its head would be many times larger than its body. The same goes for ocelots, which are already tiny, delicate mobs to begin with. ✖

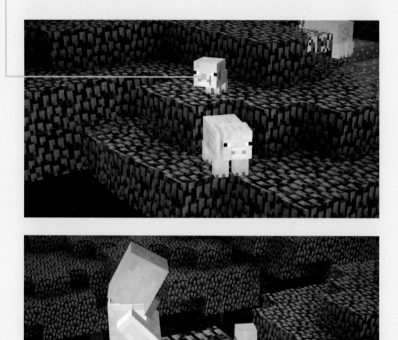

Until version 1.4, chickens would only accept wheat. That changed to wheat seeds, melon seeds, pumpkin seeds, and Nether warts. This made sense, because chickens are omnivores and eat compost. After 1.8, this was changed to only wheat seeds, and I don't understand why. ✖

Seed 1

The spawn point is in a small village, near a blacksmith with some cool items. In the southeast, at the edge of the desert, there is an impressive mountain range containing small caves, lakes, waterfalls, and lava streams. Just exploring this mountain range would take a considerable amount of time; there's a lot of variety here.

Seed 2

2107564565349426305
IN VERSION 1.8.1

You will probably spawn in the water, but you'll find a huge mushroom biome close by. Using a bowl with a mooshroom gives you mushroom soup, so with the mushrooms and mooshrooms you find here, you're set for life. The biome is interspersed with small hills and surrounded by a large body of water. There are smaller islands nearby and larger islands farther on, similar to survival seeds. A water temple can be found at these coordinates: x=240, y=60, and z=270.

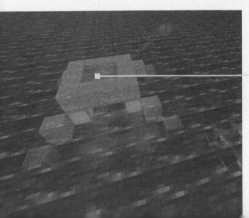

Although the seed generates a lot of water, the mushroom biome, islands, and water temple are pretty cool features.

Seed 3

-1480351183376464763

IN VERSIONS 1.7 AND 1.8

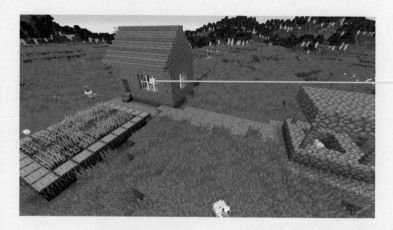

A villager lives near the spawn point in a small house with a well and a horse, surrounded by trees and mountains. Usually, villagers spawn in groups in a village, but this one lives all by himself, with no friends around. You can barter with this villager: 26 paper for an emerald; one book and 21 emeralds for an enchanted book. This is the only villager in this world. It's a very simple but funny little seed.

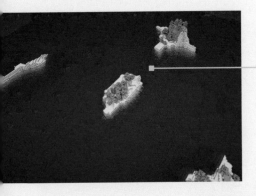

This world is mostly water. There is no real mainland, only two small islands that provide a real survival challenge. Like in SkyBlock, there are only a few resources: wood, dirt, sand, and sugarcane.

There is a water temple at these coordinates: *x=50, y=60,* and *z=300.* Fight the guards if you dare. This is not a seed for comprehensive equipment or incredibly beautiful landscapes. You are pretty much on your own, with only a few mobs around. Surviving here is a real adventure.

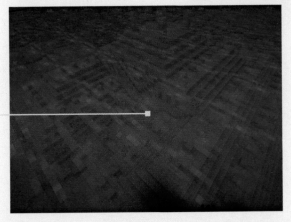

Fact 61

SQUIDS AND BATS ARE THE ONLY PASSIVE MOBS THAT CAN'T HAVE CHILDREN

Once in a while, you'll see bats, and even if you watch them for a long time, they won't breed. At least you don't *see* if they breed, because there are no baby bats. Bats are mammals, too. They should be able to have children. :=

Fact 62

SUNFLOWERS ALWAYS GROW TOWARD THE EAST

In Minecraft, sunflowers always grow in the direction of the rising sun: east. They follow this rule in real life, too. That's why they're called sunflowers.

In Minecraft, the sun still rises in the east and sets in the west, but the sunflowers do not turn their heads to follow the sun. They always

face east, even when I look in a different direction. It's much easier to press *F3* to determine which way is east, but if you want, you can fetch a sunflower instead.

Fact 63

YOU CAN REMOVE THE SUPER SECRET SETTINGS WITH F4

Super secret settings were added to Minecraft so players didn't have to download shaders. However, I still think shaders are much more beautiful, and the super secret settings never really replaced them. There are several optical changes hidden in the super secret settings.

One makes everything look circular, and another flips Minecraft upside down. In total, there are about 20 different settings. When I wanted to be rid of them, I changed one at a time until the game was back to its original state, but you can make it easy on yourself and press *F4* once. This deactivates the super secret settings and puts Minecraft back to normal. ✷

Fact 64

Sponges existed in very early versions of Minecraft but were later removed. Since version 1.8, they are back, but only in creative mode. Sponges absorb water from their environment and become wet sponges. You can dry a wet sponge by placing it into the upper slot

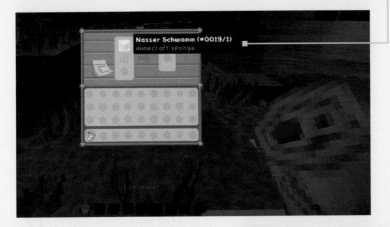

of a furnace and filling the lower slot with a bucket of lava. The furnace uses the lava as fuel, and the sponge dries. You can use alternative fuels if you wish, but it makes the most sense to use the bucket, since it will collect the water from the sponge. ✖

Fact 65

If you place the skull of a wither skeleton and a white banner onto a crafting table, you can craft a white banner with a black skull (though the banner will still be called "white banner"). That looks

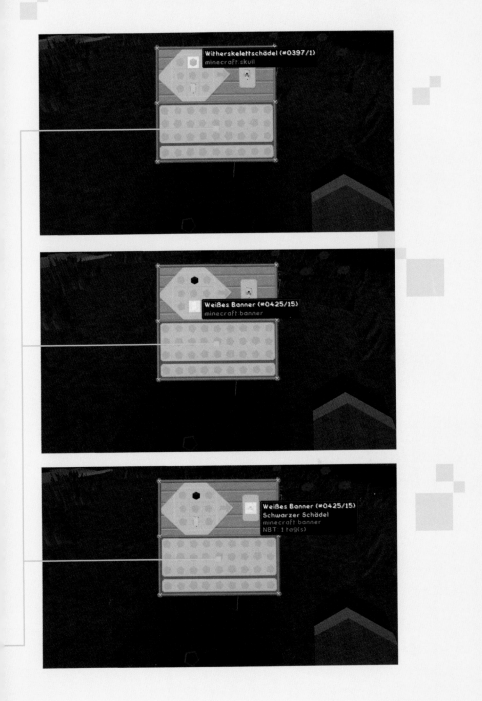

147

pretty intimidating: The wither is a boss monster, and using its head on a banner should inspire some respect.

It's difficult to find a wither skull, so making the banner isn't easy, but once you have it, you can build yourself a pirate ship. ✕

WITHER SKULLS ARE DROPPED BY WITHER SKELETONS—LIKE NORMAL SKELETONS, BUT STRONGER AND BLACK.

Fact 66

SOUL SAND PARTICLES AND MOB-HEAD PARTICLES ARE THE SAME

On the surface of soul sand, you can see wavering heads—souls, I assume, since it's already part of the name. The Minecraft developers must have thought that if you kill a mob and destroy its head, you destroy the mob's soul, as well. Here you can see a direct comparison. When I destroy them both, I receive the same kind of particles. It would be confusing if sand particles came out of a head, though.

Besides, mobs from the nether can survive on soul sand, at least until version 1.7.5. Therefore, everything is a lie. The soul is really located in the heart. There should be heart sand. ✖

Fact 67

YOU CAN WALK ON WATER BETWEEN BLOCKS IF YOU SPRINT

Blocks where you have a farm growing must be separated by water so the plants can grow. While sprinting, you can run lengthwise on this water block, regardless of how wide the trench is. Here I sprint over it in the exact middle and make it. This won't work if you're running skewed, because your path over the water block would be longer.

Check it out yourself if you don't believe me. I've tested it in version 1.8, and it works. ✖

My Favorite Maps

3: SKYBLOCK

SkyBlock is a very sparse survival map. You start on a small island in the sky with only a few blocks: some dirt blocks, one tree, and one chest with items. With these few items, you have to survive and complete several tasks. I stumbled onto this map when it was tested by some American YouTubers, and I tested and recorded it right away. This resulted in a small series that petered out after a few episodes when I got bored.

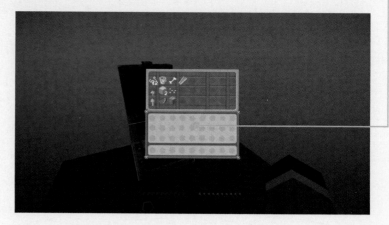

2: GTA MAP BY N11CK

GTA V is a giant world that takes 20 minutes to cross by car. N11ck's goal is to rebuild the entire map:  the docks, the airport, and even

N11ck on YouTube:
www.youtube.com/TheN11ck

his own apartment. You can imagine how much work this is for Niick and his team. They are still working on it, but even now, it's clear this will be the biggest, best, most detailed GTA map in Minecraft.

N11ck is always open to visitors
and crafting help:
Niick.net

1: IMPERIAL CITY

This isn't as big as the GTA map, but it is finished. Imperial City is full of antique buildings, temples, stadiums, rivers, and marketplaces. It resembles Rome in antiquity, but I don't think Rome was really the model. It's a grandiose project with a lot of love for detail, and it certainly deserves the grand prize.

Mods

MINECRAFT IS A VERY CODE-FRIENDLY GAME, meaning that every player who downloads the game can make changes to it. They can modify textures of existing blocks, change characteristics of the game, and add new monsters or blocks. These changes are called modifications—mods, for short. The Minecraft community has a huge modder scene that publishes a ton of mods for everyone to download.

THE LUCKY BLOCKS MOD adds only one block: the lucky block. Each time this is mined, it spawns something different. I could fall into lava and die, or spawn 100 chickens and hear nothing but clucking, or absolutely nothing could happen. The surprise is what makes the Lucky Blocks Mod cool.

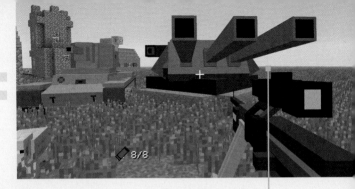

THE FLANS MOD is the exact opposite. It doesn't add just a single block but a plethora of items. This is the biggest mod I have ever seen: weapons, airborne vessels, motorcycles, cars, tanks. You can interact with all of them. You can sit in a helicopter and shoot things or grab a weapon and hunt animals. The Flans Mod has been around for a while and is expanded and improved regularly.

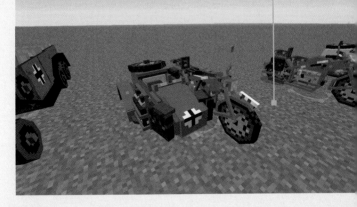

Fact 68

FLOWING WATER AFFECTS ROCKETS

Starting from the ground, rockets take off vertically. When messing around with them, I noticed that when they are caught in flowing water, the current side-tracks them, making them fly a little bit sideways. ✖

Fact 69

THE WORLD IS DARKER
ON SOUL SAND

We've learned a bit about soul sand: It's made of souls, has the same particles as a mob's head, and until a short time ago allowed zombies to survive during the day. In addition, I've noticed that clouds in the background appear darker when you stand on it. I've always imagined soul sand to be like something from *Harry Potter*, because the faces on the blocks remind me of Death Eaters. Also, in *Harry Potter*, when the Death Eaters flew to the Millennium Bridge in London, the sky grew darker, like it does on soul sand. ✳

DID YOU KNOW?
IN SPECTATOR MODE
THE WORLD IS DARKER WHEN
YOU FLY THROUGH BLOCKS.

**YOU CAN SUMMON
AN INVISIBLE HORSE**

This fact is very mysterious. The command *Isummon EntityHorse
~ ~ ~ {Variant:7}* spawns a horse that seems invisible but also isn't
really there. When you hit or shoot the horse, you can hear it taking

damage. You can even ride it. But there is no way to make it visible, even in spectator mode where you can see all blocks (even invisible ones).

How to spawn an invisible, mysterious horse:
/summon EntityHorse ~ ~ ~ {Variant:7}

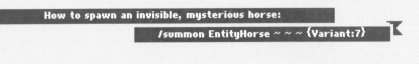

Fact 71

WHEN YOU HIT WITH A MAP, IT BRIEFLY ROTATES BY 90 DEGREES

The moment you swing, the map turns 90 degrees counterclockwise. This isn't really helpful, since the map doesn't stay in this new position. On the other hand, it's probably a good thing, since the map shows which direction you are looking, so you need to use it properly.

Fact 72

RECORDS 11 AND 13 SHOULD BE PLAYED AT THE SAME TIME

In Minecraft, there are several different records that play a variety of songs and sounds. Number 11 sounds like someone breathing while walking over gravel. Number 13 sounds like echoing cave noises. Separately these sounds don't make sense, but when played on two jukeboxes simultaneously, it sounds like someone exploring a cave. ✂

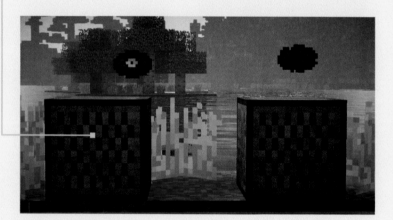

Fact 73

RECORD PLAYERS CAN FUEL A FURNACE

After testing the record fact, I needed to get rid of my jukebox. I didn't have a cactus on hand, so I tested whether a jukebox could be used as fuel. I placed it in the lower slot, and it fueled the furnace without an issue, smelting my iron ore into ingots. This surprised me. A record player is made from wood, but you should never be able to use it as fuel. It has to be crafted from wood in the first place. Still, it is possible. ✖

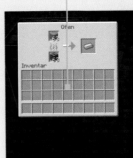

Fact 74

ARROWS ACTIVATE WOODEN BUTTONS, BUT NOT STONE BUTTONS

In addition to shooting mobs, arrows can also be used to activate redstone circuits. Wooden buttons will be activated when shot. Stone buttons will not. The screenshot clearly shows the wooden button pressed in by one pixel, while the stone button stays the same, at two pixels.

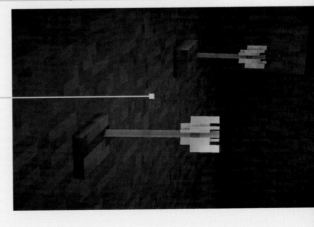

This can be useful for adventure maps, when you need to press a button 60 feet away to momentarily open a door next to you. If there is a wooden button, you can shoot it to activate the redstone. ❖

Fact 75

HOW TO STACK ARMOR STANDS
ON TOP OF ONE ANOTHER

Armor stands are entities, which means you can stack them, even when they are equipped. You can see in the screenshot that I have decorated an armor stand with a gold chestplate, leather helmet, and iron boots. On top, I placed another block and another equipped armor stand, turned in a different direction. On a third armor stand, I used chain armor. If I destroy the blocks in between, the armor stands will fall on top of one another. You can use this to create interesting things. For example, you could equip several armor stands with gold armor and twist them so that when stacked,

they create a golden circle. If you place a yellow-colored beacon under the armor stands, it looks like a sunflower beaming into the sky. ✖

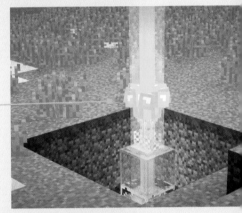

Fact 76

The ender dragon can destroy almost any block—as you can see in the screenshots—but not endstone, obsidian, or bedrock. Endstone is the End's primary material. If it could be destroyed by the ender dragon, nothing would be left before long. Obsidian is one of the strongest blocks in the game, and takes a very long time to mine. Bedrock is the lowest layer of the world. If the ender dragon could destroy that, the player would fall out of the world.

But even these blocks can't protect you from the ender dragon, who can fly through endstone, obsidian, and bedrock without having to break them.

When I started playing Minecraft and I didn't know my way around, I tried to finish the game anyway. At the time, the ender dragon and the End didn't exist yet as we know them today. I only defeated the ender dragon in the Mega Project, where several YouTubers went to the End together. ✖

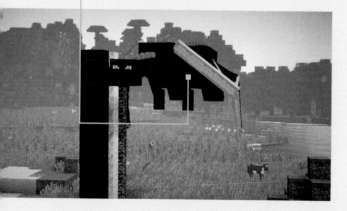

HOW TO EXCHANGE ITEMS

This simple trick allows you to exchange items in your inventory quickly and easily. Move your cursor onto the item you want to be in a different slot. Then, press the number (1—9) of the slot you want the item to move to. If there is an item in this slot already, the two items will swap positions. If the slot is empty, the first item simply moves.

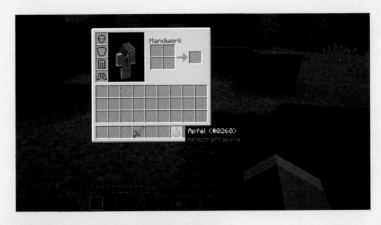

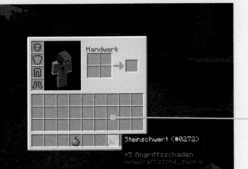

For example, if I have a stone sword in slot 4 and an apple in slot 7, I can select one of the items with my mouse—in this case, the apple—and press 4 on my keyboard. The apple and stone sword now switch positions.

Facts About Me

1 I'VE USED THE SAME MICROPHONE SINCE THE BEGINNING
The audio quality in my first videos was terrible. It became
better over time, but not by upgrading the microphone.
I picked up some extra equipment: mixing console,
compressor, equalizer, sound card, and amplifier. If I ever
decommission the microphone, I'll sign it and raffle it off.

2 I COLLECT STICKERS TO
DECORATE MY LAPTOP
At least now it has some aesthetics.

3 IN THE DRUGSTORE, I'LL BUY
WHATEVER SHAMPOO I AM
STANDING NEXT TO
Shampoos are all alike, just with
different marketing strategies.
I just grab what I see at first
glance. The same goes for
toothpaste and soap.

MY FAVORITE COLOR IS ORANGE
WITH BLACK

4

5

FOR A LONG TIME, I USED A NORMAL DESK LAMP FOR LIGHTING
Like the one from the Pixar logo. I tried to simulate a second soft box with it.

I HAVE SEVERAL BINDERS FILLED WITH RECEIPTS, COLLEGE STUFF, FESTIVAL TICKETS, ETC.
I file away small paper scraps, receipts, parking tickets, and similar stuff. In two years, I'll be able to look back and see what I did on any specific day.

6

7

EDITING IS WHAT I LIKE MOST ABOUT YOUTUBE
There is nothing better with YouTube than sitting down in the evening to edit a vlog. Editing is the heart and the soul of the video. It gives it a personal touch and should only be done by the YouTubers themselves.

I LIKE PLANNING AND GIVING PRESENTATIONS

8

When anyone in school asked for someone to give a PowerPoint presentation, I always volunteered. I love to plan, create, and give speeches. Plus, they were always extra tasks that couldn't lead to bad grades.

I THINK PURPLE IS THE COOLEST COLOR OF MY FINELINERS

I got myself a Fineliner pack a while ago. For exams in college, I have written abstracts using a different color for each topic. I wrote best with the purple pen.

FOR YEARS, I'VE ONLY USED GRAPH-PAPER WRITING PADS

Writing and calculating on graph paper works, but doing math on lined paper is difficult.

I LOVE TO PLAN MY DAY, BUT I NEVER STICK TO IT

I stick to mandatory appointments, but everything else always moves around.

I HAVE A THERMOS IN MY ROOM THAT IS SOLELY FOR DECORATION

The plan was to fill it with coffee or tea in the mornings, but I never have the time. I prefer staying in bed. So it just stands as decoration next to a wine bottle, which is also just there for decoration.

I HATE XBOX CONTROLLERS

There are Xbox people and PlayStation people. I belong to the latter. I'm just accustomed to the PlayStation controller, and the Xbox controllers seem really weird.

13

I ONLY EAT WHOLE-GRAIN TOAST

I feel like I'm living healthier this way, even though it's not true.

14

HALF A YEAR AGO, I BOUGHT A FAMILY PACK OF PAPER TISSUES, AND I HAVEN'T USED HALF OF THEM

Going to a pharmacy or drugstore while you're sick is like going shopping for food when you're hungry: You can never get enough. At the time, I was suffering from hay fever, like I do every year. Now I have a whole drawer of paper tissues. I always have enough. Just let me know if you need some.

15

16

IN BAD WEATHER, I TEND TO BE MUCH MORE PRODUCTIVE

When it's raining outside, you have to stay inside, where you have to be productive and deal with stuff.

Fact 78

Most people know that you can improve your swords with different enchantments. Looting causes mobs to drop more items when you kill them. Sheep normally drop one block of wool and raw mutton. A looting III sword can give more meat but not more wool. After killing eight sheep, I have eight blocks of wool and twenty-four raw mutton. To get more wool, you must use shears, which creates three blocks of wool per sheep. ✖

Two items with depleted durability can be crafted into a single item with increased durability. This is generally recommended, since otherwise, both items will be destroyed. However, you should avoid using enchanted items, since they lose their enchantments when used on the crafting table. You'll end up with one item that is much more durable but is no longer enchanted.

Using the anvil, the weaker of the two enchantments will be preserved. For example, an unbreaking I sword combined with an unbreaking II sword creates an unbreaking I sword with increased durability. If there's no anvil on hand, use both swords to their respective ends instead of losing the enchantments. ✄

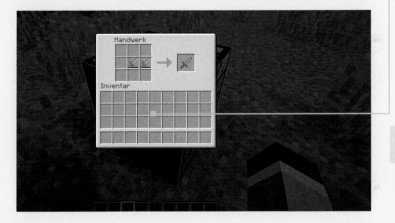

Fact 80

SKELETONS CAN'T SEE THROUGH VINES

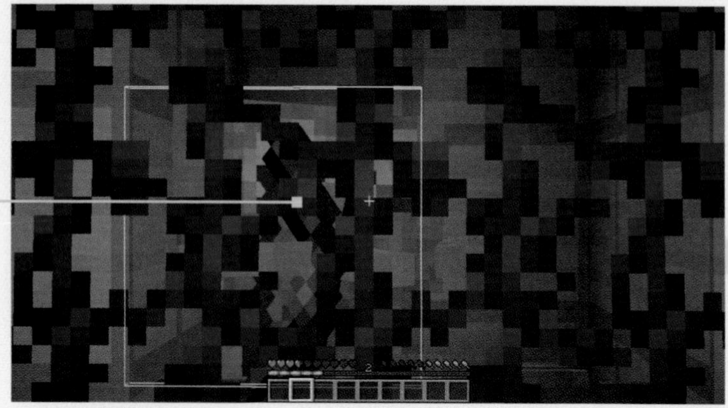

To skeletons, vines are like a solid block—like iron, for example. They can't see through them, don't know I am behind them, and don't shoot. In the second screenshot, you can see the skeletons start shooting as soon as I remove the vine. If I put the vines back or they grow back naturally, the skeletons will no longer notice me. So if you want to keep some skeletons in your house, put them behind vines and they won't lay a finger on you.

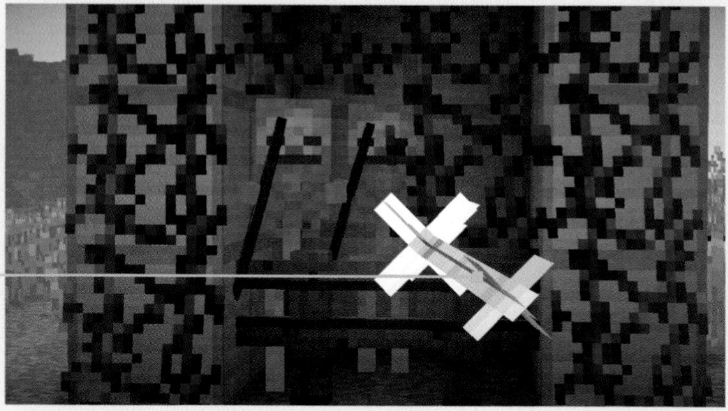

For example, if you are killed by skeletons while chat is open, this text appears: "ConCrafter was shot by a skeleton." Now you are officially dead. You have no more hearts, the skeletons stop shooting, and the world pauses. However, you can still write in chat as long as you don't leave it. The instant you do, the death screen appears, and the only way to continue is to click the respawn button. ✕

Fact 82

YOU CAN SHOOT ARROWS WITH A SWORD!

Normally, you can only shoot arrows with a bow. However, there is a small bug in creative mode that changes the rules. To do this, you must exchange a sword and a bow in your inventory using your keyboard—as we discussed earlier. In creative mode, the sword inherits the characteristics of the bow. Then when you use the sword, it shoots arrows at the same time. ✂

Fact 83

**MONSTERS BURN DURING
THE DAY, EVEN BEHIND GLASS**

Though monsters can't see or attack me from behind glass, they still
burn in sunlight. You'd think glass would block sunrays if it limits
their view, but oh well. You'll just have to live with it—which I'm sure
is not what the mobs want to hear. ✖

Command 6

New weapons

Builder: MaximCraft24

URL: http://pastebin.com/raw.php?i=8BRQRnsb

Command 6 is long, so you'll need a command block again. This will create a machine, and if I click on the "Get Items" sign, I get mighty squid bombs, anvil bombs, anvil-removal tools, fire armor, unstoppable boots, instant firecrackers, bomber bats, and firework arrows.

The fire armor is a chestplate that creates small flames around me. The unstoppable boots create several different effects. The mighty squid bomb creates a squid that spins wildly, flies up into the air,

178

then tumbles down and explodes. The anvil bomb creates a ton of anvils that fall from the sky. You can remove these anvils with the item "remove anvils." The instant firecracker creates a dog that detonates immediately and kills everything nearby. The bomber bat flies around randomly and drops lit TNT. The arrows create an effect similar to fireworks.

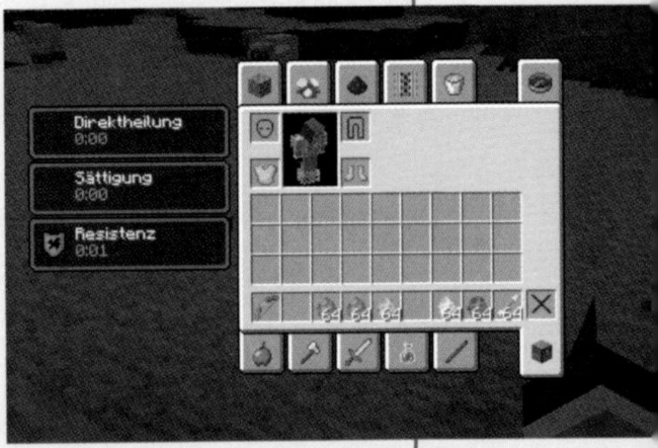

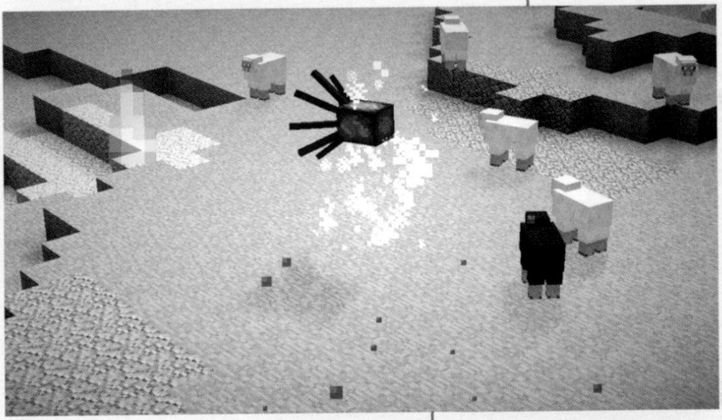

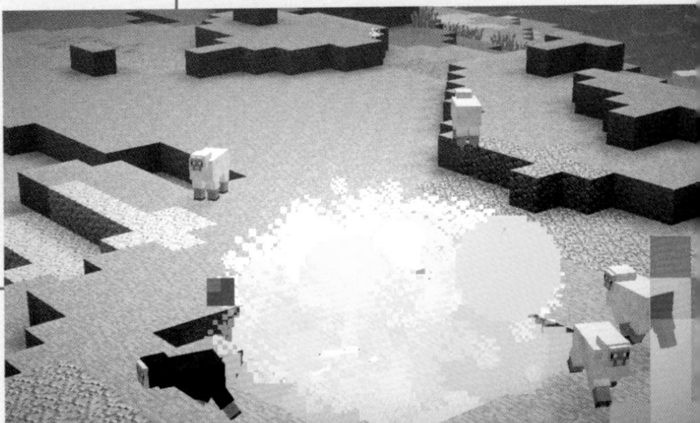

Command 7

How to turn off the spreading of fire

You can use this command when you are alone in the world and just activated natural disasters but don't want a firestorm to destroy all the forests. Usually, this function is set to *true*. Turning it to *false* stops the spread of fire, though it doesn't remove the fire itself. ⌗

Fact 84

If you mine an ice block, it turns to water and flows out over the surrounding blocks. However, if you mine an ice block with nothing beneath it, the ice block disappears without leaving the water behind.

I don't know why this is the case. I suppose it would be strange if water floated in the air, and I imagine this is too complicated to remove, but I don't know the exact reason. Tough luck for the ice block. ✖

DID YOU KNOW? ONE ICE BLOCK GIVES THE SAME AMOUNT OF WATER AS ONE WATER BUCKET.

Fact 85

THE KNOT OF A LEASH STAYS ON THE FENCE WHEN ITS ANIMAL DIES

When you leash a horse to a fence, a knot appears. If the horse is attacked or killed, the line falls to the ground, but the knot stays attached.

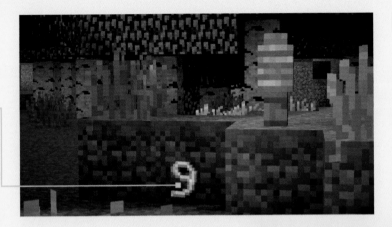

The knot will stay even if you build onto the fence. It will only disappear when you try to interact with it. That's a pity. I like the fence with the knot much better. ✖

Fact 86

A BABY CHICKEN GROWS UP AFTER 20 MINUTES OR 64 WHEAT SEEDS

Baby chickens can't lay eggs. To do that, they need to grow into hens, which happens automatically after 20 minutes. If you don't want to wait that long—20 minutes is a full day and night—you can feed it 64 wheat seeds. Eating so much causes it to grow up right away.

Fact 87

Level 256 is the highest you can build. You can change this with mods, but in vanilla Minecraft, you can't go any higher, even with commands.

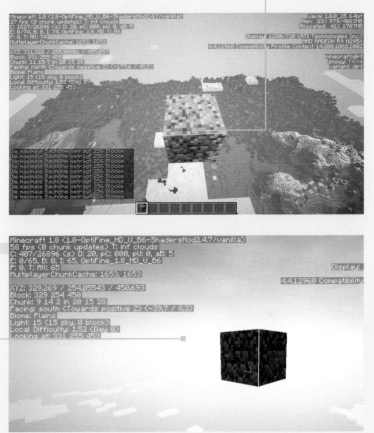

This block is on level 254. In version 1.8.1, I can't place dirt blocks on any side or on top, but I can attach levers on all sides. Why? I have no clue. ✖

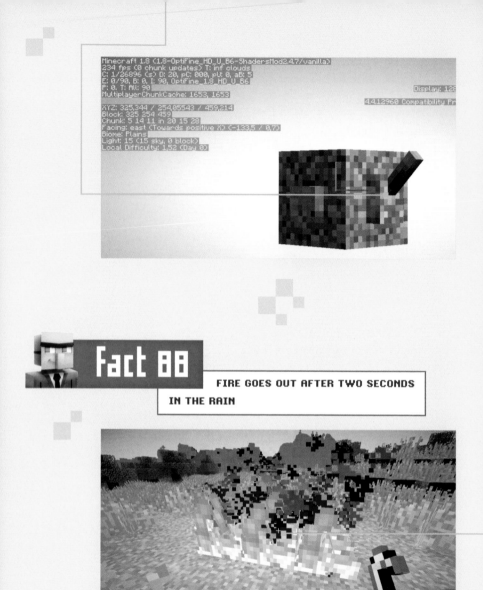

Minecraft 1.8 (1.8-OptiFine_HD_U_B6-ShadersMod2.4.7/vanilla)
234 fps (0 chunk updates) T: inf clouds
C: 1/26896 (s) D: 20, pC: 000, pU: 0, aB: 5
E: 0/90, B: 0, I: 90, OptiFine_1.8_HD_U_B6
P: 0. T: All: 90   Display: 123
MultiplayerChunkCache: 1653, 1653
                                                       4.4.12960 Compatibility Fr
XYZ: 325,344 / 254,05543 / 459,214
Block: 325 254 459
Chunk: 5 14 11 in 20 15 28
Facing: east (Towards positive X) (-133,5 / 0,7)
Biome: Plains
Light: 15 (15 sky, 0 block)
Local Difficulty: 1,52 (Day 0)

Fact 88

FIRE GOES OUT AFTER TWO SECONDS IN THE RAIN

In real life, this would depend on the size of the fire and the intensity of the rain. In Minecraft, it doesn't matter. In normal weather, without precipitation, fire burns normally, jumps between blocks, and burns out after a while. During rain, fire won't spread and goes out after two seconds. ✂

What Do You Like About Minecraft?

PXLWLF

I used to be incredibly interested in technology and watched a lot of tech videos on YouTube. At some point, one of my favorite tech YouTubers uploaded a Minecraft video. I had no idea what I was seeing, but I liked it a lot and downloaded it. I played for two days using a free trial and had a lot of fun right away. After the trial ended, I simply had to keep playing, so I bought the game. Your creativity is constrained to cubes and a limited selection, but I'm always fascinated with getting past these restraints. Plus there are the different game modes, like PvP, which make Minecraft more attractive and stop it from becoming boring.

Justin on YouTube:
www.youtube.com/PXLWLF

Rotpilz

Minecraft was recommended to me by a friend. I started playing Minecraft Classic, which you can play in a browser to get a feel for what this game is about, what to do, and what the game even is. After a while, I discovered that Minecraft also comes as a complete game, with blocks you can actually mine. I liked this a lot better than Minecraft Classic, because it gave me more freedom and nearly unlimited opportunities to let my creativity run wild. I especially love building redstone circuits, which became possible through a lot of updates in recent years. You can use it to construct gorgeous traps and all kinds of killing machines.

Felix on YouTube:
www.youtube.com/Rotpilz

GommeHD

I knew the basic principles of Minecraft from videos but was convinced it wasn't the right thing for me. At a LAN party, some friends persuaded me to explore Minecraft with them. They showed me how to use the crafting formulas, which was great, and I learned a lot through my own exploration. I'm still addicted to this day; I still get a kick out of it. Before discovering Minecraft, I almost exclusively played games with a fixed storyline, focused on the plot with a clear ending. Empire Earth was a really big thing, as well as Stronghold, which I still think is smoking hot. What I love about Minecraft is the unlimited worlds where you can simply exist, where you can run, run, run, run without ever reaching an end. You constantly discover new things.

GOMME RUNS HIS OWN NETWORK. YOU'LL FIND IT AT GOMMEHD.NET

Gomme on YouTube:
https://www.youtube.com/user/GommeHD

Luca

For me, Minecraft is about the inspiration to create something. I feel Minecraft is perfect for me, especially because I was a huge Lego fan: I never followed the manuals but just dove right in. Lego kits had a limited number of building blocks, but there are no limits in Minecraft—you have an infinite number of blocks. This boundlessness fascinates me.

I love games where you decide a lot for yourself, where you don't have some stringent story line you have to follow monotonously. In Minecraft, you don't follow the game; the game follows you. For example, say I walk somewhere and build my house on the water, then zombies come and attack me. If I build a house on a hill and illuminate everything, no zombies show up. I define this myself.

For me, that is what's best about Minecraft: You have the option to do everything the way you like. Nothing is predetermined. Other games have limitations. In Settlers, you can construct a sawmill, but only in a few places, and you can't decide how it looks. In Minecraft, there are only blocks, and you are free to do what you want with them. You can blow up the world or plant beautiful flowers everywhere. Whatever you prefer.

Fact 89

**MOBS DON'T CATCH FIRE
IN THE RAIN**

When I set fire to the block under a mob in the rain, it will only burn while the fire is lit. After two seconds, the fire goes out and the mob stops burning. It isn't possible to light a mob directly—they don't catch fire while it's raining. Also, monsters can spawn during the day if it's raining, because the rain stops the sun from burning them. ✕

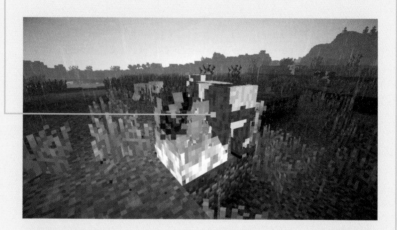

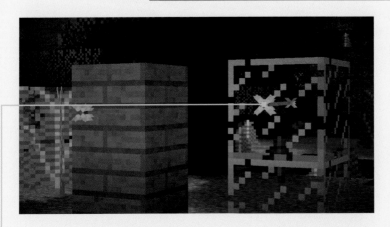

At first, I thought this only worked with transparent blocks like glass and leaves. Now I've tested it with wood, dirt, and other blocks, and from what I've seen, you can collect arrows from the opposite side of any block. Because the arrow is stuck into the block, the distance between it and the player is less than one.

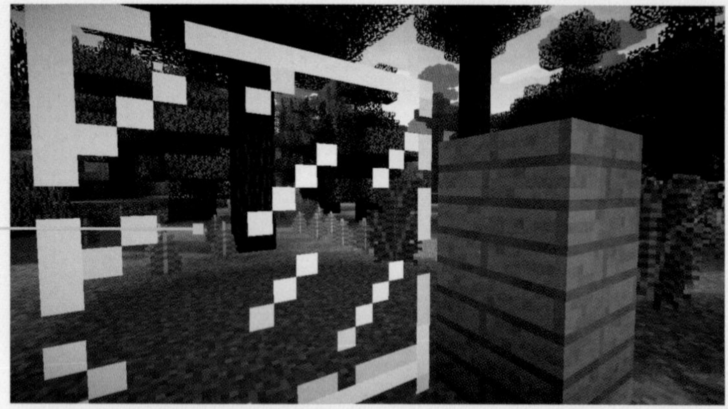

This is a bit strange; normally you can't collect items from behind a block. However, in a PvP match, you can use this as a little cheat: If you're hiding behind a wall, you can collect any arrows they fire without giving up your cover. This is great for my PvP strategy!

Fact 91

TNT BLOCKS DON'T IMMEDIATELY CATCH FIRE IN LAVA

To test this, I placed a TNT block into a 3x3 lava field, where it sat unchanged for a long time.

To me, this is weird. You can set fire to TNT directly, create fire next to it, trigger it with redstone circuits, or explode TNT around it. All of these cause TNT to explode very quickly, but placing it in lava doesn't. It is what it is, but I can live with it.

Fact 92

ORANGE SHEEP! PURPLE SHEEP! GREEN SHEEP! MANY-COLORED SHEEP!

Most sheep have white wool. With dyes, you can color the wool to red or yellow, for example. Like with colored glass on beacons, you

can mix colors by mating two sheep of different colors. In this case, we combine red and yellow into an orange sheep. Black and white sheep create a gray baby sheep.

That's pretty cool, because you don't have to look for matching colors. You can mate any two sheep you find. When the baby sheep grows into an adult, you can mate it with another sheep for even more color combinations. ✖

Fact 93

DOGS ARE HEALED BY EATING ROTTEN FLESH

When players eat rotten flesh, they'll get the hunger effect for several seconds. You can see status effects in the inventory or recognize them as particles around the player. The hunger effect turns your hunger bar green and makes it deplete faster, so you should only eat rotten flesh in an emergency. Plus, it doesn't help as much as steak or raw beef.

Dogs' life points are healed with food, and you can use rotten flesh without their suffering the status effect. Maybe they like the taste; they seem to be fine with it. ✖

To see this, you have to run into him and take a screenshot at the right moment. If you do, you'll be able to see the insides of the snowman and see a face made of small black dots. This is similar to my skin: Under my villager mask, I wear the head of a spy from Team Fortress 2.

As a player, you can put a pumpkin on your head to protect you from endermen. ✖

Command 8

Captain America command

This command adds Captain America and his armor. The command creates a machine, which prompts you to download a resource pack. Diamond armor is transformed into Captain America's armor and now gives you effects: speed, haste, and jump boost. The diamond

sword transforms into Captain America's shield, which you can use to block or hit mobs as you would with a diamond sword. With the Q key, you drop the shield, like any other item, but if you stay within a radius of 10 blocks, it will fly back like a boomerang, killing any surrounding mobs.

Personally, my favorite superhero is Iron Man, also an Avenger. The catastrophe in his latest movie was his fault, the arrogant jerk. ✖

Command 9 — Flying creeper

Builder: ConCrafter

Command: /summon Creeper ~ ~ ~ {Riding:{id:Bat}}

This command spawns a flying creeper. Well, it's not really a flying creeper but a creeper sitting on the back of a bat. This is another use of the riding command, which you've learned already. Flying

creepers still blow up like normal creepers, though they kill the bat in the process. ✖

Command 10 Hawkeye

Builder: TheMinecraftAvatar

URL: http://pastebin.com/SRjzGfXL

THIS COMMAND ONLY WORKS IN VERSION 1.8.3

Activate the command block and you'll see it working right away,  once again creating a machine.
But for now, that's all that happens. The Hawkeye command forces you to get active and craft the items on your own: a special bow and matching armor. Hawkeye's bow and armor are "S.H.I.E.L.D. issued" and indestructible. S.H.I.E.L.D. is the organization that oversees the Avengers. Hawkeye's armor gives the

status effects of speed and saturation. If you wear both at the same time, you can use the bow and—depending on what item is in your ninth slot—shoot special arrows. TNT creates exploding arrows, ender pearls create a kind of grappling hook, and glowstone dust creates fire arrows. ✂

YOU'LL FIND A PRECISE
EXPLANATION AT
THEMINECRAFTAVATAR:
WWW.YOUTUBE.COM/
THEMCAVATARAANG456

Command 11

Morphs command

Builder: MrGarretto

URL: http://bit.ly/1K4YvpO

This command creates a machine, which yet again doesn't do anything at all unless you know the command's effect: In addition to its normal items, a killed mob can drop a morph egg. When I throw this morph egg on the ground, I transform into a pig I can control. If I hit the ground beneath me with a sword, I hit and kill myself. This is the morphs command, which works with all animals. ✖

Command 12

Skeleton horse

Builder: ConCrafter

Command: /summon EntityHorse ~ ~ ~ {Type:4}

This command spawns a skeleton horse, which doesn't exist in the normal game. It emanates strange, almost electronic sounds. It won't attack, but it can't be tamed, either. It only drops experience when you kill it. ✖

210

Fact 95

Sure, you can just slap a torch on a wall, but using a frame and anvil creates a much cooler fixture. Start by placing the torch on the wall as usual. Place the frame behind the torch by aiming at the block behind the torch. On this frame, place an anvil, then turn it using right-click. This combination looks like a real torch holder and is much cooler than just placing a torch normally. ✖

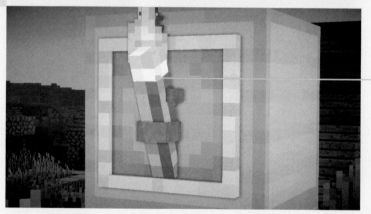

Fact 96

IF YOU DROP AN ANVIL FROM A HIGH PLACE, IT WILL BE DAMAGED

The durability of an anvil degrades from use. Over time, a normal anvil turns to a slightly damaged one and later becomes very damaged. Unlike other falling items, like sand, an anvil can be damaged by dropping it. Each time it is dropped, its durability is reduced: normal to slightly damaged, slightly damaged to very damaged, and when a very damaged anvil hits the ground, it will be destroyed. ✂

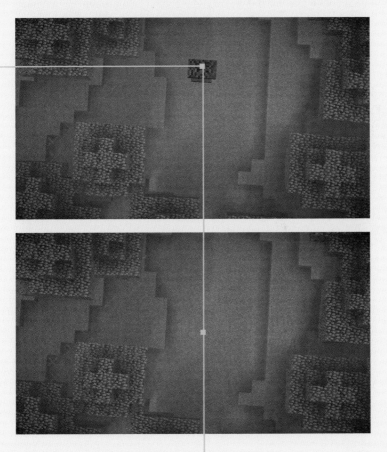

Fact 97

Using the command */summon LightningBolt*, you can create lightning. Wherever it hits, water will turn transparent, allowing you to see all blocks underwater. Lava—like dirt, sand, gravel, and other ground blocks—does not turn transparent.

This comes in handy during creative mode, when you want to find a block you dropped, where ore is, or where squids are swimming. ⁕

The lightning-bolt command: */summon LightningBolt*

215

Fact 98

WATER CAN FLOAT ABOVE TORCHES

I don't know why anyone would want to float water in the air, but with this little trick, it's possible. It's not enough to place a torch on the ground and pour water over it; the torch will disappear and the water will fall. Place one torch per block over an area of 3×3 blocks—nine in total. Then place an ice block above the torch in the center. Gradually, the torches will warm up the ice, and when the ice melts, the water stays floating in the air. It won't spread or destroy the torches,

IF YOU ARE IN A HURRY, A LIGHTER CAN SPEED UP THE PROCESS SLIGHTLY.

as long as the torch directly beneath it isn't removed. You can replace all the other torches with blocks and enjoy your floating water. ✖

216

Fact 99

EMPTYING A BUCKET MAKES IT LOSE ITS ENCHANTMENT

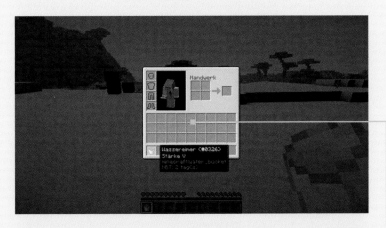

You can enchant nearly any item, including a bucket. For example, I used an anvil to enchant my bucket with strength V. If I'm in the mood, I can beat up mobs with this bucket or do whatever else. But

as soon as I empty the bucket, the block changes, and I lose the enchantment. Even if I fill it again, the enchantment won't return. It doesn't make much sense to enchant a bucket in the first place, but I still think it's a bit stupid that the enchantment disappears. After all, you're enchanting the bucket, not the water in it. If you play PvP often, don't extinguish yourself with an enchanted bucket or use the water in any way, or you'll lose the magic. ✂

Fact 100

We've already learned that you can deactivate the super secret settings with *F4*. Using *F5*, you can change to third-person mode, which also switches off the super secret settings. Even after switching back to normal, the super secret settings stay deactivated. If, for some reason, you can't remember *F4*, using *F5* to change views will do the same thing. ✄

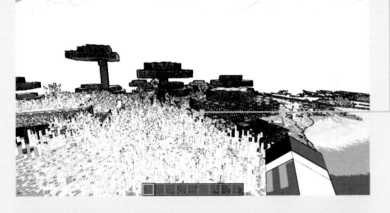

My Favorite Games

THESE ARE THE GAMES I PLAY MOST. They're not in any particular order, because they're pretty much equal.

First comes `Minecraft.` It would be weird if this weren't included, since my YouTube channel is based on it. When you are with friends, you can't play Minecraft very well, so I mostly play Minecraft when I am bored. It offers something for everyone: You can fight mobs or just relax and build.

I played in a soccer club for a long time, still play with friends, love to watch soccer on TV, and I think soccer is just a great sport, so FIFA definitely has to be on this list. Of all my games, I play `FIFA` most in my free time. I own every release since 2006, along with the specials for the World Championships, the European Championships, and FIFA Street. I have a dozen versions already, and there is a new one every year.

On my cell phone, I play almost exclusively Soccer Physics. It's an iPhone game with only one button, which makes the character jump and kick the ball. That's even how the developers describe it: Press the button to control your character. You really don't even control the character, and the game is just an epic fail, but it's really funny and great to fool around with! My friends and I play Soccer Physics quite often: while we're sitting on the train bored stiff or when we're out to eat and killing time waiting for the food.

GTA V must be included. When you're hanging with friends in the evening, you don't want to share one cell phone to play Soccer Physics. The same goes for FIFA, which you can only play two at a time without joining others in a team. You can create a rule in GTA: When one player dies, it's the next player's turn. In our circle, the first one flies to the top of a skyscraper and jumps off, the next grabs a car and drives down a hill very fast, then someone grabs a Jet Ski and speeds through Los Santos.

If I were only allowed to play one game, I would definitely choose Minecraft. Everything is possible with the help of mods: playing soccer, building Super Mario levels, or walking through the world of GTA V.

My Favorite YouTubers

MR BEN BROWN.COM

Ben Brown on YouTube:
www.youtube.com/benbrown100

MR. BEN BROWN

Ben Brown lives near London, travels around the world, and is a daily vlogger—he films one day and uploads it the next. Through his lens you see something new in the world every day. He is incredibly nice and sympathetic, very sociable, and never grumpy. I've followed Ben Brown for many months—nearly years. I'd like to switch lives with him for a day.

Casey Neistat on YouTube:
www.youtube.com/caseyneistat

CASEY NEISTAT

Casey Neistat is an American filmmaker. He lives in New York and is married with two children. He became a father at 17 years old and had a second son 17 years later. For a few months, he has been up-loading daily vlogs. Each one takes a different form. Sometimes he talks about a single topic, sometimes he answers questions, and sometimes he just records his day. In most of the vlogs, he talks about his past: how he nearly died once, or how he did a back somersault on a bicycle with a half-pipe, or how he crashed a car while producing an advertisement for Mercedes-Benz.

MARKIPLIER

Markiplier is one of the biggest gaming YouTubers worldwide. He uploads a video nearly every day covering a range of games, and on average, he is very good. His excitable antics separate him from other users; you always get what's on his mind, and there's always something to laugh about.

Dan the Director on YouTube:

www.youtube.com/DanTheDirector1

DAN THE DIRECTOR

Dan the Director is from Cape Town, South Africa. He produces time-lapse and slow-motion videos about the life stories of other YouTubers. His movies are among the highest quality you can find on YouTube or other platforms like Vimeo. This, my friend, is YouTube on another level. I wish there were more YouTubers like him, who use all of their available creative opportunities.

Vacation Stories

IN 2000, I SPENT A WEEK ON VACATION WITH MY FAMILY IN MAJORCA. EVEN AS WE ARRIVED, IT WAS ANYTHING BUT RELAXED.

We flew in from Paderborn, a two-hour flight, and were already approaching Palma when the pilot pulled the plane up again. There was a full thunderstorm over Majorca, causing the pilot to cancel the landing sequence two or three times. I didn't notice any of this on the plane and only learned of it from my dad after landing. Now, when I ask him why he doesn't fly anymore, he points to this flight. The next day, the sun was shining as if nothing had happened.

In the hotel, they told us there was a jellyfish plague, and a few people had nearly died from stings. While swimming, I struck out with my legs and brushed a jellyfish. I was scared of all of them, and I immediately thought of the dangerous ones. Luckily, it wasn't dangerous, but it still hurt.

The weather changed constantly throughout the week. Sometimes we had bright sunshine, then we were back to the rainstorm of the century. One evening, we were driving a rental car and had to cross a road with a steep decline. There was so much water pouring across the road, we weren't sure we could cross without being carried away. My dad gunned it across the road and we made it, but not without sliding down the hill a bit.

A YEAR AGO, IN THE SUMMER OF 2014, I WAS WITH MY FRIEND KRANCRAFTER AT THE NORTH SEA.

We joined a soccer tournament, walked through the supermarket, and played table tennis—just what you do during vacations. During all these activities, we repeatedly ran into a boy, maybe 10 or 11 years old, who seemed to live in the same hotel as us. A few days later, we were sitting in front of the playroom next to a box of toys, seat cushions, and the like. Suddenly, we saw a cell phone held around a corner, and someone took a picture of us. We knew the phone belonged to the young boy, and when we asked him about it, he said, "I didn't take a picture of you. I took a picture of the box."

Fact 101

Do cats and chickens get along with each other in real life? At my grandmother's, the chickens were always scared of the cat, even though the cat never harmed them. Chickens are afraid of a lot of things, and they run away when you approach. What sissies!

Ocelots are the stand-ins for cats in Minecraft, and it seems they can't stand chickens, either. If an ocelot gets into your chicken coop, he'll attack them all, one after the other, so it's best to keep them separated. ✕

DID YOU KNOW? OCELOTS CAN'T STAND CHICKENS BUT GET ALONG PERFECTLY WELL WITH DOGS.

Fact 102

TAMED WOLVES DIE AFTER THREE HITS

A normal untamed wolf dies after one hit from a diamond sword. However, if I tame the wolf that has full health, I can hit him twice without killing him. By becoming his master and giving him all my affection, I have tripled his life points. �

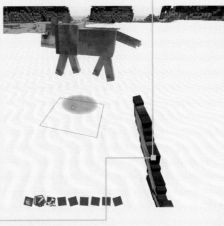
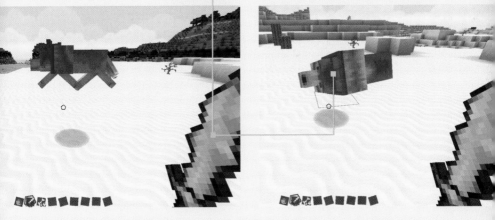

Fact 103

Creepers become charged when they're hit with a lightning bolt. This happens only rarely in the normal world, but they can be spawned with commands. Before exploding a charged creeper, I place a zombie nearby, and when the explosion kills it, its head drops.

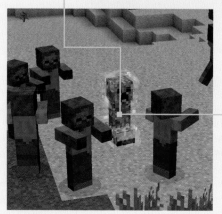

228

There's no real use for zombie heads yet, but you can put them on your head and walk around. The zombie here looks at me, thinking, *What's up with you?*

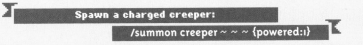

Spawn a charged creeper:

/summon creeper ~ ~ ~ {powered:1}

Fact 104

TEXT THAT FLOATS IN THE AIR

In adventure maps, you often see signs floating in the air: "Here's your checkpoint." With a small command, you can spawn this in your own world. The main component is an armor stand, which is an entity that, as we learned previously, can be rotated in any direction. Place your text between the quotation marks after CustomName—like "Hello!"—and the text will be readable from any

direction. In game mode 3, you'll see the armor stand exists, but it's invisible. I think it would be cool to use this if you have several sections on your farm. Instead of writing "Hello!" you give each sign the name of a plant; for example, "Carrots" in front of the carrot field. ✄

Text that floats in the air:

/summon ArmorStand ~ ~ ~

{CustomName:"Hello!",CustomNameVisible:1,Invisible:1,NoGravity:1}

Fact 105

As we discovered before, it snows in Minecraft above the clouds. With the command */tp 0 100000 0* I can teleport myself to an altitude of 100,000. At this level, snow already starts to shake. Higher up, the snow turns to threads, which get longer and thicker the higher I go. If I teleport myself higher, in the area of 1 billion, the snow disappears entirely, and Minecraft starts acting crazy. ✖

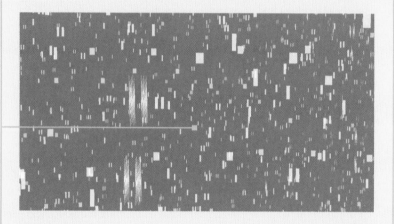

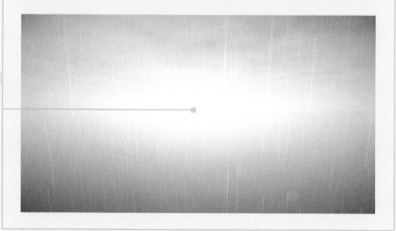

Teleport yourself
to any location by coordinates: /tp x y z

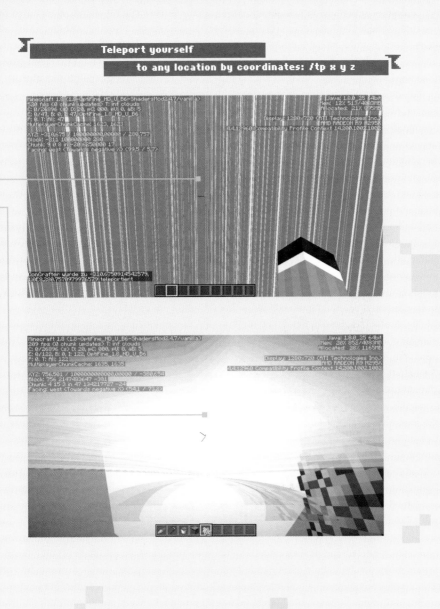

233

Fact 106

Spiders are peaceful during the day unless you attack them. At night, spiders change their behavior and start trying to kill you. If I try to run away, they follow me. If I set down enough torches, the brightness calms the spider down.

If you always carry torches during your nightly excursions, you can keep spiders at bay. It won't help with other mobs, which stay evil, but the spiders will change. ✖

234

Fact 107

MINECRAFT CRASHES
IF YOU PRESS F3 + C

Definitely check this out yourself. Keep pressing and releasing *F3 + C*, and after about 10 seconds, Minecraft will crash. First, the dirt screen appears, then the launcher prompts an error message. I took a screenshot for you: "Uh-oh, it looks like the game has crashed. Sorry for the inconvenience. :(." So don't fall asleep on *F3 + C*; it will lead to a bitter end. ✄

Hi there, my dear friends,

I still don't fully grasp what's happening right now.
My own book . . . wow. When I started out on YouTube
a while ago, my goal was to maybe entertain a
hundred people with my videos, and now I hold my
own book in my hands. This is so unbelievably cool.
This handwritten thing here—I have no clue what
to say! :D I just would like to say I'm incredibly

grateful. This might sound a little weird, but you little rascals really grew on me. :D.

I'd rather scribble five more pages of thoughts right now, but the book has to end at some point. :) It was nice of you to keep reading to here, and I hope you liked it!

ConCrafter

This way to
the secret video
in the book

ConCrafter :)